Pearson's Prize

PEARSON'S PRIZE

Canada and the Suez Crisis

John Melady

THE DUNDURN GROUP
TORONTO

Copy-editor: Andrea Waters
Design: Alison Carr
Printer: TRI-GRAPHIC Printing Limited

Library and Archives Canada Cataloguing in Publication

Melady, John

    Pearson's prize : Canada and the Suez crisis / John Melady.

Includes bibliographical references and index.

ISBN 10: 1-55002-611-9
ISBN 13: 978-1-55002-611-5

    1. Pearson, Lester B., 1897-1972. 2. Suez Canal (Egypt)--History.

3. Egypt--History--Intervention, 1956. 4. United Nations Emergency Force.

5. Canada--Foreign relations--1945-. I. Title.

FC621.P4M45 2006   962.053092   C2006-902682-3

1 2 3 4 5   10 09 08 07 06

Conseil des Arts du Canada   Canada Council for the Arts   Canada   ONTARIO ARTS COUNCIL CONSEIL DES ARTS DE L'ONTARIO

We acknowledge the support of the **Canada Council for the Arts** and the **Ontario Arts Council** for our publishing program. We also acknowledge the financial support of the **Government of Canada** through the **Book Publishing Industry Development Program** and **The Association for the Export of Canadian Books**, and the **Government of Ontario** through the **Ontario Book Publishers Tax Credit program** and the **Ontario Media Development Corporation**.

Care has been taken to trace the ownership of copyright material used in this book. The author and the publisher welcome any information enabling them to rectify any references or credits in subsequent editions.

J. Kirk Howard, President

Printed and bound in Canada
Printed on recycled paper
www.dundurn.com

Dundurn Press
3 Church Street, Suite 500
Toronto, Ontario, Canada
M5E 1M2

Gazelle Book Services Limited
White Cross Mills
High Town, Lancaster, England
LA1 4XS

Dundurn Press
2250 Military Road
Tonawanda, NY
U.S.A. 14150

In memory of John C. Garrett
Educator, mentor, friend

CONTENTS

ACKNOWLEDGEMENTS

I WAS A UNIVERSITY STUDENT when the Suez Crisis took place. Perhaps for that reason as much as any other, the seriousness of the event had a special impact on me, as it did on my classmates. All of us were of draft age, so none of us knew if we were going to be conscripted to fight England's fight. After all, in the wars of the past, that was what had happened.

Fortunately, the matter was resolved, and while nuclear weapons were armed and ready, none were used. The world relaxed, and one man from one nation was singled out as the person who did more than anyone else to resolve the problem. That was why Lester Pearson was awarded the Nobel Prize for Peace. I was thankful to Pearson, and I decided that someday, I would write about what he had done to save the world from war. However, I never dreamed that the gestation time for this account would be fifty years.

But even after all that time, I still needed the help, wise counsel, and the suggestions of many before the manuscript became a reality. At this time, I would like to thank them. First of all, Kirk Howard, my publisher, who offered his advice, direction, and resources in deciding to publish these words. I am also grateful to so many others who assisted me at Dundurn. Among them are Beth Bruder, Tony Hawke, Barry Jowett, Ali Pennels, Andrew Roberts, Jennifer Scott, and especially Andrea Waters, who has read every word of the text, edited it, and made my efforts as presentable as she could.

As they have been in the past, librarians Jeanette Finnigan and Reg

Thompson were again very helpful. So were many others at the Central Reference Library in Toronto, as well as Rodney Travers-Griffin and Bill McMaster in the same city. Goderich, Ontario, bookstore owner Tom Fincher gave me excellent advice and marketing suggestions. So did several individuals in Ottawa, particularly those who assisted me at Foreign Affairs Canada and at Laurier House.

In Britain, the staff at the Imperial War Museum were of help, as were the knowledgeable personnel that I dealt with in Egypt, particularly at Port Said and Cairo. Unfortunately, I no longer know your names, but I was impressed by your breadth of information and your ability to impart it.

In New York, Michael Kovrig at Dag Hammarskjöld Place was generous with his time, assistance, and direction. Shadrack Mbogho showed me around both the Security Council and the General Assembly at the United Nations and patiently answered every question I asked in both places. At the UN as well, Veena Manchanda was of great assistance in the search for the photographs that I needed.

Closer to home, Dan McMillan and Carolyn Parks gave me both direction and the benefit of their advice. In London, Ontario, Elaine Ruttan and Mike Dobson helped in the photo editing and cropping. Joe Vick saved my neck when my computer hard drive died, while John Snell listened to my complaints about deadlines and writing-related difficulties but never showed annoyance.

And lastly, but most important of all, my wife, Mary, who was always encouraging and supportive of the project. The fact that she also admired Lester Pearson was an additional bonus.

John Melady
Seaforth, Ontario
May 2006

INTRODUCTION

OVER THE YEARS, I have been lucky enough to have met, talked with, or shaken the hands of several of our prime ministers. In fact, I have even played golf with one of the more recent residents of 24 Sussex Drive. And even though such contacts were often fleeting, each of these men left an impression on me. While I might not have voted for all of them, I respected all of them. I respected them because through their own initiative and deep-seated drive, they had reached the pinnacle of political success in this nation. They all held the most powerful, most important, and at times, I suppose, most frustrating job imaginable. Not all were successful. In fact, one or two were washouts as prime minister. On the other hand, I know that even *they* did the best they could with the talents they had. For that reason, I thank them for trying.

Yet of all these leaders, one stood out for me before I met him, when I met him, and since I met him. In fact, Lester Pearson was, to me at least, one of the finest prime ministers we have ever had. With his self-effacing, modest demeanour, his finely tuned negotiating skills, his clarity of vision, and his integral honesty, he brought humanity and honour to the top job in the land.

I met Pearson only once. It was during an election campaign, and because of a scheduling fluke, he had arrived some fifteen minutes early for a speech. His handlers seemed quite frustrated by the problem and at a loss as to how to use the extra time. Because I had hoped to meet the prime minister anyway, I happened to be standing nearby when a local official who knew me called me over. He introduced me to our distinguished visitor and then disappeared. I was obviously nervous and not sure what I should say, but Pearson noticed my discomfort and immediately put me at ease. He asked me what I did, where I worked, and what I thought of the party's prospects in the local campaign. Then I mentioned the United Nations and his time with the organization.

The Prime Minister listened, and, with what I took to be a rather wistful smile, said, "I loved it there." Then we shook hands and he was called away. A minute or so later, he was giving a stump speech on a small-town stage that was light-years removed from the Speaker's dais in the General Assembly in New York. And while I remember being thankful that this great man had been able to bridge the gap, I also think that being prime minister was not his preferred role. Fortunately for us, and for civilization, he was doing his other job when the Suez Crisis caused the world to pause.

CHAPTER ONE

To Save the World

EACH TIME THE PILOT ATTEMPTED to land at Ottawa that night, the runway disappeared. So did the terminal building, the lights of the city, and the hope of a timely arrival. A wild winter storm had obliterated everything, and even though ground crews fought to keep the airport open, the plane from New York was still not down.

The captain of the big, four-engined DC-7 came in as low as he dared, strained to see the Tarmac, and, because he could not, pulled up and went around again. Once, twice, three times. Finally, on the fourth approach, the runway lights flickered into view, and the aircraft was on the ground. All souls on board were immensely relieved.

The brief stop in Canada's capital was highly unusual on this Saturday, December 7, 1957. Normally, planes operated by Scandinavian Airlines did not come to Ottawa at all. They flew to New York and returned to either Oslo, Norway, or Copenhagen, Denmark. Flights to Oslo, with a refuelling stop in Scotland, were on Wednesdays, Thursdays, and Saturdays.

The plane that arrived in the Ottawa storm was one of 338 manufactured and nicknamed the "Seven Seas." The Douglas Company, which built the machine, boasted that it could fly 110 passengers to any destination in the world. The engines were propeller-powered, and average speed was between 330 and 400 miles per hour. Those who flew it regarded the aircraft as being as reliable as any in the air.

Awaiting the plane's arrival that night at Ottawa were three passengers. Two were well-known; the third less so. The least familiar was Mary

MacDonald, but she was the executive assistant to the man everyone in the terminal seemed to recognize. Maryon, the man's wife, was with him.

The sixty-year-old gentleman with the beaming face and jaunty bow tie was Lester Bowles "Mike" Pearson, at the time a lowly member of the Opposition in Parliament in Ottawa. But Lester Pearson was much more than an ordinary member of the House of Commons. Until his Liberal party had lost a federal election just six months earlier, he had been what was called at the time the Minister of External Affairs for Canada. Six years hence, he would be his nation's fourteenth prime minister.

But now, on this cold December night, he was just three days away from becoming the first and only Canadian ever to win the Nobel Prize for Peace. That was why he, Maryon, and Mary MacDonald were at the airport. They were about to fly to Norway, where Pearson would receive what is arguably the most prestigious award in the world. The man had certainly earned the accolades of his fellow citizens, who basked in his reflected glory.

In the days and weeks prior to his leaving for Oslo, papers across Canada and far beyond its shores praised Pearson's actions and agreed that he was deserving of Nobel recognition. As expected, his fellow Liberals in Ottawa were the most enthusiastic about this recognition for one of their own. But the good wishes were not theirs alone. Even the man who seemed forever jealous of Pearson and who found fault with so much of what Pearson did offered his grudging congratulations. John Diefenbaker was now prime minister of Canada, albeit with a somewhat precarious minority, but he felt he had to be positive about Pearson's achievement.

Doing so was difficult for the prairie populist, however, and never more so than on the day the prize was announced. That was back on October 14 — coincidentally, the same day Queen Elizabeth, who was in Ottawa at the time, read the Speech from the Throne to open the Canadian Parliament. Never in the history of the nation had this been done before. And with his unstinting admiration for all things royal, Diefenbaker revelled in the grandeur of the occasion. Much to his surprise, however, shortly before Her Majesty was about to make the journey from Rideau Hall to Parliament Hill, word of Pearson's prize became public. Diefenbaker was chagrined.

The news was a pleasant shock for Pearson. "My father was in a rather drab basement office at the time, and a reporter called him," Pearson's son Geoffrey recalled. "The caller may have been Charlie Lynch, who was a good friend, but I'm not sure now. Anyway, whoever phoned told Dad he had won the Nobel Peace Prize. At first, Dad laughed, thought the call was a joke, and refused to believe it. But it turned out to be true."[1]

Within minutes, Pearson's little office was packed with well-wishers. Scores of individuals, from custodians to cabinet ministers, showed up, shook his hand, hugged him, and congratulated him on the achievement. The phone rang incessantly as the news spread. Reporters from all the major papers called, and breathless radio and television bulletins were aired and repeated.

The news almost overshadowed the visit of the royal couple to Canada. After all, Pearson's Nobel Prize was a more upbeat item than the news that Prince Philip was out duck hunting in marshes along the Ottawa River, some thirty miles from town. He had been up at five that morning and, with his private secretary and two Royal Canadian Air Force officers, had been knee-deep in muck as he participated in the shoot. By mid-morning, he was out of his hip waders and back at Rideau Hall, bragging to the Queen about the eight ducks he shot. No one knows whether she was amused or not.

But while Philip was playing sportsman, Pearson remained in his office as Mary MacDonald scoured Ottawa in an attempt to locate Mrs. Pearson so that Mike could relay the good news to her. MacDonald's search came to naught, however. "We couldn't find her because she had gone to get her hair done someplace new, not where she ordinarily went. We didn't know where she was."[2] Maryon Pearson did not learn of her husband's good fortune until she returned home an hour or so later.

"When my mother got the news, she was quite skeptical," Geoffrey Pearson remembered. "She was a very practical person, and she tended to keep my father in his place. I was in Paris when the news broke, and I did not get a chance to talk to Dad right away."

Patricia Hannah, Pearson's daughter, was at her home in Milton, Ontario. "I found out about the prize in a call that morning," she explained. "My husband, Walter, and I had two little babies then, and I was at home looking after them when the phone rang. It likely was my father who called, but I am not really sure anymore. But when I heard the news, my first reaction was disbelief. I was surprised, astounded, amazed, thrilled, and very proud. I remember having every one of those reactions."[3]

The congratulatory hubbub was still taking place in Pearson's office when the official word came through from the Norwegian Nobel Committee. The confirmation led to more broadcast updates, while newspaper reporters reworked the stories they were frantically composing.

But, as expected, the spotlight shifted to the journey the royal party made through the streets of Ottawa. The thirty-one-year-old Queen Elizabeth rode with Prince Philip in an open landau on the two-mile trip from Rideau Hall to the centre block of the Parliament Buildings. Four black horses pulled the open carriage while forty-eight RCMP officers on horseback escorted the sovereign. The Mounties wore their red dress uniforms for the occasion, and an estimated five hundred thousand people lined the streets as the procession passed. An untold number watched the spectacle on television. Fortunately, the early autumn day was sunny and warm.

The Queen read the Throne Speech in the red-carpeted Senate Chamber, where every seat was taken. And while there was probably some worthy content in the document she was given to read, the Queen's deportment, dress, and presence got most of the attention. As soon as the thirty-seven-minute speech had been delivered, the royal couple returned to Rideau Hall.

That same evening, a gala dinner for 115 of the nation's elite was held at the Governor General's residence. Again, the Queen's every glance, gesture, and smile was reported by the press. Her "Maple Leaf of Canada" dress got as much coverage as a flood in Valencia, Spain, that left a quarter of a million people homeless. Both accounts made the front pages the next day.

By way of comparison, the presence of Prime Minister John Diefenbaker was sparsely mentioned, an oversight that surely must have been a blow to his inflated ego. In fact, so many who were there wanted to congratulate Pearson that he often became the centre of attention instead of Diefenbaker. Pearson later mentioned this in his rather jocular description of the event: "At the state dinner at Rideau Hall, I got almost as much attention as the new Prime Minister."[4]

And soon, he would get even more.

The next day, October 15, Canada's national newspaper, the *Globe and Mail*, placed news of Pearson's Nobel win not only on the front page but on the second, sixth, and tenth as well. An editorial entitled "Deserved Distinction" summarized the paper's point of view. The editors reminded their readers that Pearson "spoke strong and clear for Canada," and because he did "his fellow-countrymen felicitate him." Most other papers reacted in kind, if without the archaic turn of phrase.

Now, ALMOST EIGHT WEEKS after the announcement of the prize, Canada's former Minister of External Affairs, his wife, and his assistant walked through the snow from the Ottawa terminal and climbed the steps into the plane that would take them to Norway.

Pearson's account of the journey is rather amusing. He recalled that the aircraft had to detour to Ottawa for him, and that because of the storm, both the landing and the subsequent departure were unavoidably late. Both a taxiway and the main runway had to be cleared repeatedly. Then he learned that because of the delay, none of those on board had eaten dinner. He and Maryon had done so during the wait at the airport. Nevertheless, feeling embarrassed and sorry for the famished passengers, they managed to put on brave faces and force themselves to eat what they could of a second meal. And what a meal it was!

"When we were finally airborne," he wrote, "it was near midnight, and they started serving this very special, deluxe, unprecedented, seven-course Nobel Peace Prize dinner. We were almost to Norway by the time we got through the last course."[5]

Naturally, because it left Ottawa when it did, the plane's arrival at Oslo on Sunday was far behind schedule as well. In fact, it did not touch down until mid-afternoon in the Norwegian capital, and because that city is so far north, the December sun had already set. Nevertheless, an official government welcoming committee was at the airport to greet Pearson. So were members of the press, officials from the Canadian embassy, and others.

As soon as the welcoming procedures ended, the Pearsons were whisked to their downtown accommodation, where they were finally able to get some much-needed rest. The next morning, they would begin a whirlwind week. For that reason, despite their long, tiring flight, a restless night in a strange bed, and a six-hour time change, both Mike and Maryon were up early.

In 1957, as today, the Nobel Peace Prize came in three parts: a gold medal, a diploma, and a sum of money. The latter item was presented first, and the recipient actually went to pick up the cheque. In Pearson's case, he was expected to call at the Nobel Institute at 11:00 a.m. for his money. He was late for the appointment — but for good reason. That was because his first experience of that first full day came as a surprise.

Prior to going to the Nobel Institute, Pearson was scheduled to go to the Royal Norwegian Palace in downtown Oslo and sign the visitor guest book. Doing so was expected to be little more than a formality, and the Canadian chargé d'affaires, J.F. Thibault, Pearson's host in Oslo, felt the ritual would take fifteen minutes at most. If he got Pearson to the signing by 10:45, he reasoned, they would still have plenty of time to make it to the Nobel office on schedule. However, the Canadian visitors had barely entered the palace when the private secretary to the King came to greet them.

Would Mr. and Mrs. Pearson please be kind enough to accompany him? King Olaf wished to see them.

The invitation was as pleasant as it was unexpected. Maryon immediately felt that her dress was much too casual for an audience with His Majesty, and then she noticed that the business suit her husband wore was rather rumpled and certainly not the formal attire ordinarily expected for such an occasion. Nevertheless, the King's command was to be obeyed.

Olaf V was a relatively new sovereign, having assumed the throne barely three months earlier on the death of his father, King Haakon. Olaf had yet to preside at an official public function, but the very next day he would be in attendance when the Nobel Prize was awarded. While the fifty-four-year-old monarch was a bit younger than Pearson, the two liked each other immediately and soon found they shared common interests, particularly their knowledge and appreciation of history and world affairs. They talked for over half an hour, while protocol officials were forced to cool their heels in another room. Now, they realized, the Canadian parliamentarian would be late for his 11:00 a.m. appointment.

In due course, however, the audience with the King did end, and the Pearsons were driven to the Nobel Institute, a classic mansion only a stone's throw away from the palace. The Institute has been at this location since 1905 and today houses, among other things, a 180,000-volume library, most of which is devoted to peace and international relations. I was there to see the place a few years ago and found that it was well worth the visit.

The principal duty of the Institute is to work with and provide supporting documents for the Nobel Committee as they select the winner of the Peace Prize. The committee consists of a five-member group appointed by the Norwegian Parliament, the Storting. The comittee not only selects the prize winner, it subsequently bestows the medal and the diploma. An official at the Institute issues the monetary award.

When Pearson arrived that day, the man who handed him the cheque was August Schou. Pearson accepted it with grace, and then, in the company of Doctor Schou, a handful of dignitaries, members of the press, and others, he toured the Institute and noted the photographs of previous winners that adorned its walls. Today, his picture is among them. By the time he was ready to leave, the press had reported that the cheque Pearson had received amounted to US$40,000. Because our dollar was worth more than the American one at the time, the actual stipend to Pearson was CAD$38,885.55.

Patricia Hannah told me her mother invested the money.

The Nobel Prize medal was awarded to Pearson at a mid-morning ceremony on December 10. The date is of particular significance. Sixty-one years earlier to the day, Alfred Nobel, the Swedish chemist who invented dynamite and a score of other things, passed away in San Remo, Italy. Never married, and with no close friends, Nobel was a strange genius who became fabulously wealthy during his lifetime. In fact, when he passed away, his fortune was "spread over ninety-three factories in nine countries."[6] Until almost the end of his life, he travelled constantly, visited his holdings wherever they were, and worried constantly about production quotas, shipping problems, and, when it occurred to him, worker satisfaction and morale. Instinctively curious and to a large degree self-educated, he spoke fluent Swedish, German, English, French, Russian, and Italian, wrote plays and poems in English, and read widely in several languages.[7]

It is somewhat ironic that the man whose main invention could and would be used destructively at times, and who always worried about such uses for it, nevertheless had a passion for peace. This fortuitous streak in his makeup led ultimately to his leaving money for the prizes that carry his name, one of which is for peace. The others are for physics, chemistry, medicine, and literature; a sixth, related award for economics was added in 1968. Because Nobel was a Swede, it was that country that first faced the problem of interpreting his wishes and allocating the money involved. His will was only a page long, and it was not easy to interpret in places. For that reason, "the brevity and ambiguities of this testament, disposing in so few words of so huge a fortune for such a variety of prizes, took its executors, and the academies and the Swedish government as well, five years to turn into a workable institution."[8]

Finally, the officials involved came to a consensus, and the first prizes were allocated in 1901. Because Nobel had decreed that it should be so, the peace prize was to be awarded in Norway, by Norwegians. The others were distributed from Sweden.

Today, the awarding of the Nobel Peace Prize is done in the Oslo city hall, but when Pearson became a Nobel laureate that day in 1957, the ceremony was held in the Aula, or great hall, at the University of Oslo. The Aula is a large, handsome, classical structure located in the city centre between the Storting and the Royal Palace. Inside, the art of Edvard Munch adorns most of the wall space.

Munch, a Norwegian artist whose best known work is his 1893 painting *The Scream*, used paint on canvas for his Aula depictions, the centrepiece of which is called *The Sun*. The art is dazzling, uplifting, and pleasant. Because *The Scream*, *The Sick Child*, and much of Munch's earlier works were brooding and tortured in nature, the lively, colourful scenes in the Aula are somewhat unexpected. On the other hand, they are reflective of the joyous occasions when the Peace Prize was awarded there.

Sadly, the Aula also has a darker past. While the paintings were removed and hidden for safekeeping during the Second World War, "the Aula was a venue for arrests and custody for hundreds of students."[9] At least twelve hundred students and teachers were incarcerated there during one of the darker periods of the Nazi reign of terror in Norway.

The fact that the Peace Prize was awarded in the same building was highly appropriate.

At the ceremony for Pearson, the chairman of the Nobel Committee, Doctor Gunnar Jahn, presented the gold medal and the diploma and explained to the capacity audience of over seven hundred why this modest, self-effacing Canadian parliamentarian deserved the prize.

Addressing the crowd in Norwegian, Jahn began by summarizing Lester Pearson's career, both before and after he became involved in diplomacy and politics. He referred to the Canadian's role in the founding of the United Nations and to his belief in that organization, which culminated in his becoming president of the General Assembly in 1952.

Doctor Jahn then turned to a situation that had shaken the world the previous year. The matter, which became known as the Suez Crisis, developed in the summer and fall of 1956. For several critical weeks, the world was on the brink of war. Egyptian President Gamel Nasser nationalized the Suez Canal, and Britain, France, and Israel attacked him because of it. Russia supported Nasser, and Soviet Premier Nikita Khrushchev threatened nuclear holocaust if the United States became involved militarily.

As expected, the matter soon became a major problem for the United Nations. Fortunately, because of the efforts of Canadian Minister of External Affairs Lester Pearson, the crisis was defused. Pearson proposed a UN peacekeeping force be sent to Egypt to separate the warring factions there and keep the peace. Because his idea was adopted, Jahn maintained, Pearson saved the world from war. For this, he won the Nobel Prize.

In his lengthy speech at the presentation ceremony, Jahn mentioned the laureate's name a total of forty-two times, summarizing Pearson's career, his political position, his role at the UN, and, finally, his contribution to humankind that led to the Nobel Prize. The repetition led to Pearson's rather witty response when he rose to offer his thanks.

As one newspaper noted in reporting the event, "Mr. Pearson spoke briefly to Jahn's speech. He started out saying that he unfortunately had not been able to understand the speech in Norwegian, but that the two words he understood seemed to crop up far too often: "They were 'Lester Pearson,' he said."[10]

The Nobel laureate then went on to express his thanks and stressed that while the prize might have been given to him, it was equally deserved by his many friends and colleagues who too laboured unceasingly "for peace and international understanding."

The following evening, December 11, the Canadian parliamentarian delivered his official Nobel Lecture to a black-tie audience in the Aula. The next day, after several courtesy calls in Oslo and some hurried sightseeing, the Pearsons left for home. On the way, they stopped in London to see George Drew, the newly appointed Canadian High Commissioner to Britain. A week after that, they were the guests of honour at a testimonial dinner in Toronto.

Through all the days of congratulations, Pearson maintained his sense of humour and his well-documented insistence on remaining rooted in the practicalities of the real world. After all, it was through his work in the real world that he had found the fame that was thrust upon him. And part of that world was, in the fall of 1956, a far-off land where sandstorms, poverty, conflict, and commerce came together in a terrifying way.

CHAPTER TWO

A Ditch in the Desert

LESTER PEARSON WON the Nobel Prize because of events in an ancient land. That land was Egypt, a country that was old before Pearson's was new. It was in the dominion of the pharaohs that a canal was built, a project that had been talked about for centuries but that was no more than a dream for a long time. That dream would become the Suez Canal. It was the culmination of the hopes and desires, the failures and successes, of people of vision through countless ages. As long as there were explorers, traders, adventurers, and those who sought fortune and fame, hope for a canal refused to die.

As far as we know today, the first proponents of such a project came up with the idea as early as the thirteenth century BC. Then, the proposed route differed markedly from what it is today. Now the canal connects the Mediterranean Sea with the Gulf of Suez by way of the Bitter Lakes and a desert trench. In contrast, the direction suggested by the ancients went from Great Bitter Lake west through excavated land to the Nile River, and thence down the Nile to the Mediterranean. In time, a rudimentary waterway was constructed, and it seems to have followed such a route.

It is known that a canal existed during the Ptolemaic era, between 323 and 30 BC. Subsequently, however, it fell into disrepair because of neglect and the forever drifting desert sand. Much later, sometime during the 98–117 AD era, Roman Emperor Trajan ordered the thing repaired, and it was again used, although somewhat briefly. When western traders realized they could access the riches of India by circumnavigating Africa, canal use ceased. Again, the dunes of the desert obliterated the dreams of men.

Several centuries passed.

With the ascent of Napoleon to the throne of France, the idea of a canal in Egypt was revived. Great men with great plans sought to make the Emperor's France the most important nation on earth. Trade expanded, commerce grew, and industrialization gave rise to prosperity, wealth, and an optimism that knew no bounds. Because trade was ever-increasing and vitally important, any way of facilitating it had to be considered. The route to India, by way of the Cape of Good Hope, was long, expensive, and often perilous. Many a ship went out and never returned. And because of storms, misadventure, breakdowns, and navigational errors, those that came back often took a long time to do it.

Because they hoped to find a more direct, faster, and safer way to move goods, Napoleon's engineers went to Suez. There they measured, calculated, and planned. A canal linking the Red and Mediterranean seas became somewhat of an obsession and, in the optimism of the time, a real possibility. Such a waterway would dramatically shrink the distance from Marseille to Madras, reduce costs, and (though this was a somewhat secondary consideration at the time) save the lives of mariners and the vessels they sailed. The dreams of old were suddenly new again.

But Napoleon's wise men were not so wise. In fact, they made a major miscalculation, and in so doing almost ended any hope that a canal would ever be built.

The water levels of the two seas to be linked are the same. However, through an oversight in measurement or an error in interpreting the numbers before them, the surveyors somehow concluded that the surface of the Red Sea was thirty feet higher than the Mediterranean. And if that was the case, breeching the land barrier between the two would result in massive flooding at the northern end. For this reason, the canal project was set aside for a time.

Then a smooth-talking, irrepressible visionary appeared on the scene. The man's name was Ferdinand de Lesseps.

The son of a French diplomat, born in Versailles, and a member of the establishment of the day, young de Lesseps was a natural optimist.

He knew in his heart that whatever he tried would be a success. This faith in himself, coupled with an ambition and energy that knew no bounds, stood him in good stead when he turned his attention to building a canal at Suez. Like his father, he had become a member of the French diplomatic corps, and he found himself stationed in Egypt.

Although he was always a citizen of France, de Lesseps lived for long periods of time in Egypt, where he travelled the country, in particular the area between the seaside city of Alexandria and the capital, Cairo. In the former, he rubbed shoulders with Muhammad Said Pasha, the son of the ruler of Egypt, who loved to spend his summers in Alexandria, where the cooling breezes of the Mediterranean provided an escape from the blistering heat of Cairo.

In due course, Said got to know de Lesseps well, and in many ways, the two became kindred spirits. Even though they came from very different backgrounds, both felt called to greatness, and each was determined to leave his mark in history. They also agreed on how they might do so.

Both believed that a canal from the Red Sea to the Mediterranean was something the world needed. The two discussed the idea, did some rudimentary planning for it, and talked it up among their friends and moneyed associates. To Said, such a canal would help restore some of Egypt's faded glory; with such a waterway, the riches of the east could be easily transported to and marketed in the west. To de Lesseps, a canal would make it easier for France to expand its influence in the opposite direction and, in so doing, make the enlightenment of the West attainable in the East. Of course, France was in competition with Britain, whose empire already circled the globe.

In July 1854, Said became viceroy, or khedive, of Egypt. At this juncture, de Lesseps saw his chance. He refined the idea of a canal and set out to convince the new ruler that now was the time to make their dream come true. As Zachary Karabell writes, "Said's support was an imperative first step, but it was only the beginning of a long, uncertain road that time and again looked as if it would end in failure."[11] From then on, "it became Ferdinand de Lesseps's canal, and he had no intention of sharing."[12] The man was not only ambitious, unscrupulous, and hard-driving, he was a megalomaniac. It would be *his* dream, *his* project, *his* canal.

And, ultimately, it was.

For months on end, de Lesseps scoured Egypt and France for the necessary funds to embark on his grandiose scheme. He also had to locate European engineers who would be able to bring his idea to fruition. Both of these elements took perseverance and more than a decade of work. In fact, from its beginning in 1854 it would take a total of fifteen years until the canal became a reality. It was opened at last in 1869. By that time, an Anglo-French company owned the canal, and Egypt and the successors to Said would gradually come to realize that they were not in control of the greatest resource in their own land.

In his almost messianic entreaties to the French, de Lesseps was able to convince a vast array of people to invest in his canal company. These ranged from his cousin, Eugenie de Montijo, the wife of Napoleon III, to scores of "small shopkeepers, cab-drivers, [and] peasants," all of whom bought shares. He "appealed to the small investor partly because he wanted to, partly because only from the small investor could he get the necessary funds without putting himself into the hands of the great banks."[13] He felt that if the banks took control, they would push him aside, and his dreams of greatness would be shattered forever.

In Egypt, thousands of fellahin, or peasants, were conscripted to do the physical work involved in the actual excavation for the canal. These men were little more than slave labourers, "made to dig and shovel and haul earth for this strange new trench through the sands." For their efforts "they were paid a few piastres a day ... and [then sent] back home, worse for wear but at least not dead." They did what they were told because they "knew they would be whipped if they tried to escape and treated roughly if they shirked."[14]

On January 17, 1863, Said died at the age of forty-one. His successor as viceroy was a man named Ismail, whose main claim to infamy was his tendency to overspend. He built palaces and parks, railways and roads, and did all he could to make Egypt and things Egyptian the envy of the world. He vastly increased military spending, had scores of lavish public buildings constructed, and quickly exhibited a taste for high living. To no one's surprise, he accumulated more and more debt, and to pay for it had to sell many of his own and his country's shares in the new canal.

The official opening was a year-long event and was one of the most lavish parties in history. There were representatives of the royalty of almost every country, along with their retinues and their hangers-on. Thousands of well-to-do people came from France, Spain, Netherlands, England, and elsewhere. French Empress Eugenie led the parade, and ships of maritime nations moved down the canal in a flotilla as grand as could be imagined. There were fireworks, speeches, dances, and more extravagant banquets than the diners had ever seen. And there was music, music of every kind and from every culture. Even the great composer Giuseppe Verdi was persuaded to write an opera for the occasion. He demurred initially, but after sufficient financial inducement he composed the work that became known as *Aida*, although it was not ready in time for the canal opening. Instead, it was performed at the Cairo Opera House in late December 1871. Verdi did not go to Egypt for the premiere.

But even though the canal was complete and revenue from it began to accrue, the Viceroy's financial nightmares continued to grow. For his palaces, his greed, and his fame, he had mortgaged his future. Six years after the first ships traversed the waterway, the Egyptian was in deep financial trouble. Reluctantly, he turned to the money men of England for help.

Up until this juncture, while British ships did travel through the canal — and in a rather short order became its principal users — the government of the day seems to have failed to grasp that the new waterway represented the shortest trade route to the Far East. In the words of Winston Churchill, "The Foreign Office had been curiously slow to appreciate this obvious fact," and in doing so "had missed more than one opportunity to control the waterway."[15]

They would not miss another.

Noting the Khedive's financial straitjacket, Benjamin Disraeli, then prime minister of Britain, stepped forward and, with the support of his country's banks, bought the Suez Canal shares for some £4 million. In doing so, Britain became the principal shareholder in the Suez Canal Company. However, as Churchill observed much later, the purchase meant that "Britain was inexorably drawn into Egyptian politics."[16] That involvement would not be short-lived.

In fact, from 1882 until 1956, when the last of the British troops that would be garrisoned in Egypt left that country, the British were closely linked with the nation on the Nile. Through the years, the canal retained its importance, and France and particularly Britain benefited from it.

Eventually, the waterway was deemed vital to the livelihood of its principal shareholder. To ensure that it would always be secure, soldiers from Kent and Northumberland, London and Leeds, would be stationed in Egypt, in particular in the Suez Canal Zone. This occupation was costly, socially unfortunate, and never without an undercurrent of rancour. In fact, it was, as Peter Mansfield describes it, "neither a happy [time] nor one of which Englishmen can be especially proud. Its unmistakable positive achievements have to be set against the British attitude towards the Egyptians which was at best a patronizing affection and at worst a contemptuous dislike. This changed very little over the years."[17]

No wonder a man named Nasser would have such an impact.

WHEN HE FIRST MADE HIS PUBLIC DEBUT, Gamal Abdel Nasser was a lowly soldier in a ragtag army. He had neither resources nor background; he was not a hero, but he was not a fool. Despite a humble family origin — his father was a postal worker — this young man harboured a burning ambition. He loved his homeland, and from an early age he decided to do all within his power to make Egypt great again. He wanted to make his nation less dependent on Britain and turn it into a player on the world stage. Whether he succeeded or not is still being debated.

Because his mother died when he was only eight years old and his father was apparently unable to care for him, young Gamal was sent to live with a succession of relatives in a variety of places. This circumstance proved to be beneficial to the man the boy became. He got to know his own country as well, perhaps, as anyone ever could. Everywhere he lived, he became one with the people there. He saw them working, worrying, and dreaming of a better life they would never have. For the most part, he saw grinding poverty, learned of its causes, and saw its effects. These people, he told himself, had to be helped, and he was determined to do so.

But the realization of his role was arduous and long.

Gamal Nasser was a shy, sensitive, quiet child who did well in school but was never what might be called brilliant. He had also a rather brooding demeanour, which, because he could spend hours on his own, reading and thinking, came across as being somewhat standoffish. It was through his reading, though, that he learned so much about his own world and of what was over the horizon. An observant and devout Muslim, Nasser's only vice as an adult was smoking.

To a degree he was self-educated. Any gaps in his schooling were filled by his all-consuming desire for knowledge and the books he devoured. He spoke and read Arabic, of course, but he was also fluent in English. "In addition to the Koran ... he read Carlyle, Napoleon, Gandi [sic], Dickens, Voltaire, Hugo, Lord Cromer (onetime British governor of Egypt), Liddell Hart, and many others."[18]

When he was a child, during his time in school and then in the army, "the British had run Egypt outright, or at least tried to do so. Then came a period when it served their purpose to rule by means of Egyptian governments but to keep them as soft and pliable as possible so that they could easily be manipulated."[19]

Nasser resented this, as did most of those with whom he came in contact. In fact, rightly or not, Britain became the scapegoat for all that ailed Egypt. When the Suez Canal had to be protected in time of war, no Egyptian was allowed near it without a permit. Even though he knew and understood this, the fact that there were places in their own country where Egyptians could not go still rankled Nasser. So did the conduct of the occupying army, most of whom liked little and cared less about things Egyptian. In fact, it was said that "for the average British soldier a typical Egyptian was a Cairo prostitute or a Port Said pimp."[20]

During his time in the army of Egypt, Nasser's resentment was not limited to the occupiers from England. He also was thoroughly disgusted with the way the Egyptian king at the time, a man named Farouk, operated. Farouk was a fat egotist who was thoroughly corrupt and widely disliked, both within the army and outside it. By war's end, he had alienated all but his cronies. Finally, led by Nasser, a group of Egyptian army officers who believed they could do better staged a coup, and the hated Farouk was suddenly out of a job. He was forced to flee the country on his personal yacht on July 26, 1952. Nasser never looked back.

The coup was both successful and controversial. Because most of the ringleaders were young, they were inexperienced and had almost no knowledge of legislative affairs, but they were confident, almost to the point of arrogance. However, they were also realistic enough to understand that in order to win over a skeptical public, a recognizable and respected figurehead should be at the fore. In this role, they placed General Mohammed Naguib. He was known, liked, and temporary. Nasser replaced him in 1954.

From that time on, in fact until his death from a heart attack in 1970, the words *Egypt* and *Nasser* had much the same meaning. During all that time, Nasser was the undisputed power in the nation. It was for that reason that he will be forever linked with what became known as the Suez Crisis of 1956. It came about because of the actions of this Egyptian soldier and the response of others to what he would do.

CHAPTER THREE

The Cause of a Crisis

WHEN GAMAL NASSER CAME to power as the first president of Egypt, there were still great numbers of British troops garrisoned in his country. They were located at several places, but particularly at a huge, sprawling, sand-encrusted compound near Ismailia. There, some eighty thousand members of the British military lived, or more correctly endured, all the while doing what they could to protect themselves from well-organized Egyptian agitators who conducted constant guerrilla attacks. At times when the soldiers were not fending off this harassment, they were repairing armament that had been sabotaged, securing equipment that could be stolen, and protecting property that was easily torched.

Few of the British were happy to be in Egypt, and even fewer Egyptians wanted them there. Nevertheless, because this was during the Cold War, the security of the Suez Canal was paramount. It had become the lifeblood of Britain, and ever-increasing shipments of Middle Eastern oil transited the waterway each year. Any breakdowns in the trade route would be catastrophic for Britain, and to a lesser extent for the European continent as well. Nevertheless, in spite of the Cold War climate, but with Nasser's continued assurances that the canal would be kept open, negotiations to end the occupation continued in Cairo, London, and Washington.

Ultimately, it would be the military point of view that would win the day. The "armed services chiefs had already come to realize that the base would be [and was rapidly becoming] militarily useless without Egyptian acceptance and co-operation,"[21] and coming to some kind of agreement with the host country would get personnel home and save millions of pounds in occupation costs. Finally, the interminable talks came to an acceptable conclusion, and an agreement in principle to remove the troops was endorsed in the fall of 1954. On June 13, 1956, the last British soldiers boarded a ship in Port Said harbour, and the occupation of Egypt was over. Nasser now had won two rounds: he had sent Farouk packing, and he was rid of the British.

But in his eyes, Egypt needed something more.

Nasser never strayed far from his humble beginnings, nor did he ever forget the poverty, deprivation, and hopelessness that so many of his countrymen endured. Egypt was a poor country whose population was increasing at a time when fewer and fewer resources existed to better the lot of many. So much of the land was unworkable, desolate, and without water. The endless sand might be picturesque, it might even hold undiscovered riches, but it would not support agriculture.

As I travelled the country researching this book, I saw what poverty is and what poverty can do. And this was not just in rural areas where peasants laboured for little, in much the same way as they had for thousands of years. It existed in the noisy, dusty, chaotic streets of the big cities as well. I saw rag-dressed patients outside a Cairo clinic, lying on blood-soaked stretchers, desperately trying to shoo flies away as half a dozen lanes of traffic roared past a metre away. And these people were the lucky ones. They had a clinic to go to.

Gamal Nasser saw the same things and dreamed he could help.

Egypt's economy is heavily dependent on the waters of the Nile, that majestic river that flows for hundreds of miles from its source in Sudan to the salt shores of the Mediterranean. In fact, to a large extent, without the Nile, there would be no Egypt. As a celebrated historian once remarked, "How precariously narrow a thing this Egypt is, owing everything to the river, and harassed on either side with hostile, shifting sand."[22]

Because the Nile is prone to flooding, vast networks of irrigation trenches have been constructed to contain the overflow. The retained water is pumped farther and farther from the river, enabling additional land to be cultivated and more crops to grow. Yet even with this expanded acreage, there never is enough to supply the nutritional needs of the populace.

It was into this reality that Nasser stepped once he took office as president. And it was with this reality that he set out to launch the largest and most grandiose project of his career. He had long dreamed of harnessing the Nile for two expanded purposes: irrigation and, to a lesser extent, hydroelectricity. In time, both would be accomplished, but Nasser would not live to see the impact of either.

But that is getting ahead of the story.

Suffice to say, once in power, Nasser embarked on a project to build a great dam on the Nile, at Aswan, in Upper Egypt. The edifice would be 365 feet high, almost 3 miles wide, and would store close to 50 billion cubic feet of water. This storage capacity, regulated and harnessed, would bring about greatly expanded irrigated acreage and electricity for an untold number of public buildings, factories, and homes. The only stumbling block was the cost.

Negotiations to finance the construction dragged on for some time, and as might be expected, the United States had an integral role in the matter. So did Britain, and the American-led World Bank. During the time the talks about the dam took place, American Eugene Black was the World Bank's president. He had much to say in the protracted consideration of the project, but U.S. Secretary of State John Foster Dulles had more. Dulles, the irascible, hot-tempered giant of American foreign policy, was never hesitant about expressing his views about the dam. He consulted others, sometimes even listened to them, but it was within his self-assured inner core that he, and ultimately he alone, decided the fate of Nasser's dam.

But what of his equally strong-willed opposite number in the endeavour?

Nasser could be just as bullheaded as Dulles, and as steadfast in the direction he intended to take. "Our role," claimed Nasser in a reference to his leadership of the nation, "as determined for us by the history of our nation [leaves] no choice, no matter what the price we have to pay."[23] He then proclaimed that it was necessary to "create a program to insure the prosperity and well-being of our country so that each and every individual might be certain of his daily bread." The big dam would play an important role in the provision of that bread.

However, another equally significant factor complicated the talks involving the Aswan project. In the world Nasser knew, the various states of the Middle East were, as they are today, ever on the edge of unresolved long-term disquiet. Such a situation had existed for years, but in Nasser's day it was complicated by the founding of the State of Israel in 1948. The creation of the state by the United Nations was the result of a long-term Zionist dream of a permanent home for the Jewish people. The move was made despite outspoken opposition from Arabs — one of whom was Gamal Nasser. He resented the existence of Israel and did what he could to see that the new nation failed. In 1948, at the conclusion of what became known as the Arab-Israeli War, the Egyptian had found himself on the losing side. As an army major at the time, he looked about him and realized that his country had been humiliated by a stronger, more organized, and better fighting force. He laid the blame for most of this debacle on the Egyptian leadership, and from that time forward determined that Farouk had to go. Finally, once he had gotten rid of the king, ousted Naguib, and assumed the leadership himself, he fully realized the magnitude of the problems he faced.

One of these was the ongoing antipathy between his nation and the Jewish state on the other side of the Sinai. In spite of the fact that Israel and Egypt had signed an armistice agreement on January 31, 1949, an ongoing series of border raids between the nations made for an uneasy peace. In addition to Egypt, other Arab states bitterly resented the existence of Israel, so much so that the raids continued sporadically for an extended period of time. Finally, "in 1955 attacks increased across the 1949 armistice lines. Fedayeen (partisans) from Gaza, Egypt, Jordan, and Syria struck towns and settlements in Israel, while Israeli commandos attacked Arab outposts."[24]

As expected, both sides in the conflict felt the need to increase their military capability. Both wanted arms, and they were not necessarily selective about where they got them. They used the excuse that they had to defend themselves from constant attack, and better aircraft, guns, and missiles were a necessity.

The border raids were numerous, and they often led to the loss of innocent lives. After each raid — from either side — there was retaliation, follow-up attacks, and more retaliation. One of the most serious instances of retaliation led to Israel's Black Arrow attack in early 1955.

In the latter months of 1954 clandestine peace talks between Israel and Egypt were underway. Unfortunately, the more militant factions on both sides had no desire to see the negotiations succeed. Then an Israeli sleeper cell began sabotage operations in Egypt. They attacked libraries, post offices, and even movie theatres in an attempt to create the impression that Egypt was not a good environment for business — particularly foreign business.

The activities of the cell members were rather ham-handed, and within a relatively short time, all were caught. Shortly after his arrest, one of the group committed suicide. Several others remained in jail, and the two alleged ringleaders were sentenced to be hanged. As Nasser was sure the whole affair was an Israeli plot to overthrow him, he refused to commute the death sentences. Despite international condemnation of Egypt, the two were executed in late January 1955.

The deaths caused uproar in Israel. Israeli founding father David Ben-Gurion assumed the role of minister of defence, while retired general Moshe Dayan took over as chief of the military, the senior soldier in the country. Together they selected a man named Ariel Sharon and ordered him to exact revenge. Colonel Sharon, who would go on in later years to become prime minister of Israel, was, at the time of his selection for Black Arrow, a tough, trained, and altogether fearless paratrooper with a reputation for ruthlessness. He was told to mount an attack in the Gaza Strip on an Egyptian army post there. "As always when Sharon was in command the number of casualties was high."[25] Reports on the tally of Egyptian deaths differ widely, but the number was somewhere between forty and fifty-six. Sharon's work was complete. The revenge taken for the two Israelis who died had been carried out in spades.

Nasser was humiliated. Faced with a crisis in his own defence establishment, the Egyptian leader realized that if he was ever going to match the Israeli capability on the field of battle, he had to have help from abroad. He knew he needed arms of all kinds, but particularly fighter planes and help in the training of pilots to fly them. At the time, France was overtly and covertly supplying combat aircraft to Israel.

35

Canada, too, had sold military hardware to both Israel and Egypt, with the majority going to Israel. In 1954, shipments of military equipment to Israel amounted to $735,574.60. That year, we sold only $296.00 worth to Egypt. The following year, total sales to both countries were greatly expanded, but Israel's share was still considerably more: $1,332,110.59 to Israel and $770,825.00 to Egypt.[26]

After the Sharon reprisal, Nasser's assessment of his nation's military capability was stark. "Egypt had at the time only six serviceable planes. Thirty others were grounded," while "tank ammunition would last for a one-hour battle."[27] He knew that two of the major powers, the United States and Britain, were not about to give him the much-needed fighter planes, so he began to look elsewhere for them. Despite the fact that Nasser regarded the presence and influence of the U.S.S.R. in the Middle East with a degree of hesitation, he felt he was boxed into a corner in his quest for arms. His predicament began to be noticed in Moscow.

On May 23, 1955, "the Soviet Union ... offered to supply Egypt with all she needed in the way of arms."[28] A week or so later, the American ambassador in Cairo, Henry Byroade, was so informed. Predictably, the Eisenhower administration in Washington was appalled, and from that time on, John Foster Dulles was more hesitant than ever about giving Nasser American money to finance his dam on the Nile.

Dulles conferred with his counterparts in Britain and at the World Bank offices, and almost immediately, the wisdom of loaning money to Nasser was questioned in all quarters. Britain and the United States decried the possibility of increased Soviet influence in the Middle East. Almost overnight, the word *Nasser* became an epithet in both countries.

Perhaps sensing what the reaction abroad would be, Nasser ended up accepting Khrushchev's arms, but on paper, at least, he made the purchase in Czechoslovakia, then a Soviet satellite. The ruse was no help to his cause, however; to Britain and the U.S., arms bought from a member state were the same as those purchased from Moscow itself. The deal brought about the cessation of Anglo-American help for Aswan.

While he may have been humiliated by the Israeli killings in Gaza, Nasser was even more apoplectic at the Americans and the British because they had killed his dream. Now he felt he had to look for a Soviet offer for his pet project.

The U.S.S.R. ultimately did offer technical support and financing for the Aswan Dam. Its construction was, at the time, the world's largest civil engineering operation. Some 35,000 people worked on it, and 451 died doing so. The dam was officially completed in 1971.

Nevertheless, when the British, Americans, and World Bank withdrew the financing for the dam during the third week of July 1956, Nasser made a decision that would have lasting reverberations around the world. He was well aware of the fact that the Suez Canal was his country's most prized asset, but he knew as well that it was also vitally important to others elsewhere. The Anglo-French consortium that owned the waterway benefited greatly from it in the form of dues paid by shipping companies whose vessels used it. Those fees, if paid to Egypt instead, would go a long way towards helping Egypt pay its bills. It was for that reason Nasser decided to announce the nationalization of the canal during a speech he would make on July 26. When he did so, July 26, 1956, became one of the most important dates in modern Egyptian history.

In the hectic days that led up to the pivotal date, Nasser held top-secret meetings with his highest officials. He worked non-stop, barely slept, chain-smoked, and worried. He was taking the biggest risk of his life, and he knew it. He and a handful of men in his top coterie not only had to put in motion their grandiose scheme, they had to convince doubters, anticipate repercussions, and maintain a level of secrecy more vital than any of them had ever known.

And they succeeded.

Nasser told the hand-picked group around him that he would go to Alexandria and make his speech there, in Manshiya Square. The speech would be carried live on Cairo radio and, as such, would be heard in the farthest reaches of the nation. But it would be listened to with particular attention in four places: Ismailia, Suez, Port Said, and Cairo. This was because in these places, where the Suez Canal Company had offices, groups of men would be waiting for a signal from Nasser to act. They were the people who had been selected to take control of the operation of the canal itself.

The leader of the small, secret group entrusted with carrying out Nasser's orders was Colonel Mahmoud Younes. He was respected, even feared, utterly loyal to Nasser, and enterprising in the extreme. It was he who worked out the plan for the canal takeover and thought through the details of the operation with the utmost skill and care. He would leave nothing to chance. At a much later date, Younes explained his method: "In order to assure absolute secrecy and obedience, I told them that one man in each group, unknown to the others, had instructions to shoot on the spot anyone who violated secrecy or failed to carry out orders. This made a hard impression. Some of them sweated."[29]

On the afternoon of July 26, Nasser took the train from Cairo to Alexandria, arriving in the port city at 4:00 p.m. There, he met with several of his top advisers, had dinner, and was ready to make his address at 7:30 that evening. By the time he walked through the French doors and onto the balcony of what was called the Bourse, where he had survived an assassination attempt two years earlier, a quarter of a million people awaited his every word. He looked out over the assembled throng and noted the senior government officials seated at the front, the secret service shadow men stationed strategically, and the crush of ordinary people who spilled into the surrounding streets. Then the President cleared his throat, stepped up to the microphone, and began to speak.

At that instant, Younes' men, in groups of five, tore open secret messages that each contingent possessed, read the enclosed instructions, and then proceeded to one of the Suez Canal Company offices. The groups had with them second sealed envelopes and had been given specific directions as to when these should be opened. Inside the second packet would be further instructions.

Back in Alezandria, Nasser made a long, rambling address in which he summarized his nation's history, enumerated the times when Egypt was slighted, explained how outsiders had harmed his homeland, and told his listeners that henceforth, the land of the pharaohs would become great again. As he talked, the President's voice sometimes rang with heroic phrases; at other times, he joked with his audience, or sounded conspiratorial and devious. At no point did he use the language of sophistication. His message was given in the dialect of the commoner, the lingo of the street.

In the meantime, the four groups who were doing his bidding elsewhere had reached their destinations and were waiting for the President to say the code words, after which they were to open the second envelope and learn what they were to do next. The code words were the name "Ferdinand de Lesseps," the long-deceased builder of the Suez Canal.

In total, Nasser's address lasted two hours and forty minutes, and when he came to the explanation of how his dream of the great dam on the Nile had been shattered by the Americans, his voice became strident, accusatory, and direct. It was John Foster Dulles who was most to blame, Nasser bellowed. It was John Foster Dulles who sent World Bank President Eugene Black to Cairo to kill the dam. Then Nasser told the crowd before him, and the four groups waiting elsewhere, about his meeting with Black.

"I began to look at Mr. Black sitting in his chair, and I imagined that I was sitting in front of Ferdinand de Lesseps."[30]

The crowd heard the name and thought nothing of it. Elsewhere, the four teams heard it and sprang into action. They now knew exactly what they had to do. In short order, Younes' men, all of whom were armed, walked into four Suez Canal Company offices and took over. They had assumed control without blood being shed or shots being fired.

The Suez Canal had just been nationalized. The French-English ownership of the facility had come to an end. From now on, it was Egypt's canal.

CHAPTER FOUR

A Question of Reaction

THE SAME EVENING that Gamal Nasser announced the nationalization of the Suez Canal, British Prime Minister Anthony Eden hosted a dinner party at 10 Downing Street, his official residence in London. There were several illustrious guests there, all of whom arrived in a succession of highly polished limousines that moved swiftly down Whitehall and then turned into the short, dead-end little street that is arguably the best known in the land. The cars glided smoothly up to #10, their passengers stepped out, and the luxury automobiles turned and purred away. Then the famous black door at Eden's home opened and each new arrival disappeared inside. By all accounts, the gathering was pleasant, the dinner sumptuous, and the conversation memorable — but the occasion would be remembered for another reason. Word of the canal nationalization came just as the guests were leaving the table.

Dining with Eden that evening were King Faisal of Iraq and his prime minister, Nuri es-Said, members of the British aristocracy, and a handful of politicians, among them Foreign Secretary Selwyn Lloyd, who would become very familiar to the general public in the weeks and months that followed. The two Iraqis were in Britain on a state visit, and Eden was well known to both. At the time, young King Faisal had not been on the throne in Iraq for long, nor, for that matter, would he continue to be. He and several family members were brutally assassinated a couple of years later. The two prime ministers had been friends for more than thirty years.

The first word of events in Egypt came in a note from the British Foreign Office, hand-delivered at 10:15 p.m. to Eden. The Prime

Minister read the communication, his face betraying a sense of disbelief and consternation as he did so. When he had absorbed the crux of the message, he decided to relay its contents to those about him.

"I told my guests," Eden explained later, "and they clearly saw that here was an event which changed all perspectives. Our party broke up early," he added, "its social purpose now out of joint."[31]

Within minutes, Eden had seen his Iraqi guests to the door, after which he quietly directed the four cabinet members present to stay behind for an emergency strategy meeting. Nasser's actions were so unorthodox, some kind of immediate response was critical. In an attempt to gain a greater consensus about what to do in the short term, other ministers and senior officials from foreign governments were called in. Among them were Jean Chauvel, the French ambassador, and Andrew Foster, the United States chargé d'affaires.

Senior members of the military were summoned, as was a man named Jacques Georges-Picot, who at the time was the Director General of the Suez Canal Company. He had been in town on business and had to leave his bed at the nearby Ritz Hotel to rush to 10 Downing. Others left West End plays, dinners, and family homes. By 11:30, as many as possible of the most important government and business representatives were present. Eden requested that they gather in the Cabinet Room at the official residence, and there the meeting began.

The Prime Minister took control right away, as he would during the historic and bitter weeks that lay ahead. He briefed those present and supplemented his remarks with clarifying details as soon as he knew them. More and more information about conditions in situ arrived at the Foreign Office, and each scrap of incoming news was made known to Eden as quickly as possible. At first, there were few details about what Nasser had actually done, apart from the general nationalization report itself.

To the men in the Cabinet Room that night, the Suez Canal was one of the most vital waterways on earth. Its operation, virtually all of them knew, was governed by an agreement drawn up in 1888. That year, in what was then Constantinople (modern-day Istanbul), an international conference signed by all the major European powers declared that the canal was to remain forever neutral and unrestricted passage through it was guaranteed to all in times of peace and war. The working title for the document was the Convention of Constantinople.

Because everyone at Eden's meeting knew the canal was supposed to remain open, they were concerned right away as to Nasser's long-term intentions and how these might impact the transport of oil. Their fears were understandable in any examination of canal usage. Harold Macmillan, the prime minister who followed Eden, wrote later that in 1956, "before the birth of the giant oil tankers, the Canal was essential and indeed the only means by which Western Europe could be supplied. Seventy million tons a year passed through the Canal, representing at least half the oil supplies of Western Europe."[32]

Because the details of Nasser's declaration were still unclear, the meeting at times came close to getting out of hand. Everyone present wanted to do something — indeed they knew they *had* to do something — but in the early information vacuum, little was actually accomplished. Naturally, the Prime Minister, although he spoke and wrote Arabic and admired Arabs in general, would never have agreed with any Arab — or anyone else for that matter — who tried to close the canal, especially one who had commandeered the facility, as Nasser seemed to have done. But there was more than this to Eden's reaction to the nationalization.

The problem was Nasser.

Eden had not been disappointed when the military coup was launched and King Farouk was driven out of Egypt in 1952, "but it was unfortunate that he took a particular dislike to Nasser."[33]

No one who knew Eden was sure when the antipathy began. Most, however, pointed to the one meeting the two had at the British embassy in Cairo on February 20, 1955. The occasion was a dinner party to which the Egyptian President had been summoned, like a common petitioner for a favour from on high. He resented the fact, and apparently never forgot it.

When the two met that evening, Eden came forward, greeted the Egyptian in Arabic, and engaged his guest in some casual conversation. The two talked of the Koran and of Arab proverbs. Eden told the President that one could learn from the wisdom that these implied. The dinner that night went well, apparently, and Eden, the ever-urbane former diplomat, was in his element. However, the elegance of the surroundings and the formality of the gathering were not lost on Nasser. Later on, he said, "it was made to look as if we were beggars and they were princes."[34]

And there was one incident that night that made Eden decidedly uncomfortable, even if it was perfectly natural and should have been expected. Nevertheless, Nasser had annoyed him, Eden would explain later, "when the husky Egyptian suddenly started holding hands ... in the Arab fashion just as photographers began taking their picture."[35] In any event, the two leaders developed a dislike for each other, and the sensitivity would remain. This was quite unfortunate when they came to face each other as adversaries following the Suez seizure and the British reaction to it.

It was 4:00 a.m. when the meeting at Downing Street finally ended, without much substantive progress. This was in direct contrast to the way events had unfolded at the same time in Egypt.

As soon as they tore open the envelopes given them, the men commanded by Colonel Younes walked into the four Suez Canal Company offices and informed employees who were there of the takeover. In Port Said, the move was particularly dramatic, given the building where the change of command took place. Once little more than a collection of huts on the sand, Port Said, the city, was built for the Suez Canal. Here the great tankers line up in preparation for their convoy passage up the canal. To do so, they pass by a large, white, two-storey building on top of which are three beautiful green domes. These cupolas, which can be seen from the moment you enter the north end of the canal, are not only striking today, they were the focal point for the actions in 1956. The operations room for canal control was in the centre dome, and the men assigned with the takeover headed for it.

The Canal Company employees working in the dome were taken aback by the arrival of the strangers and the suddenness of their entry. But when they saw that the newcomers carried guns and meant business, the workers made no protest. They were told they would not be harmed in any way, as long as they stayed where they were and went on with their work. Under no circumstances were they to be the cause of any disruption of traffic through the waterway.

This condition was one that Nasser himself imposed. Because the British and French would be strongly opposed to the control takeover, so much so that they might even go to war over it, he was determined to limit their objections. The canal was to be kept open and normal passage through it was to continue unheeded. To that end, he not only took control of the company's offices, but he "imposed martial law in the Canal Zone, and forbade all employees of the Company, including foreigners, to leave their jobs."[36] By issuing this decree, Nasser was particularly astute. In the promulgation of "a flawlessly legal document putting forth Egypt's right to nationalize, Nasser was beating the West at its own game. He was staying scrupulously within the law."[37]

This last point was hotly debated by the group Eden had assembled in London. Some of those who were there were sure that Nasser had broken every law in the book, indeed, had committed an international outrage. Others were not so sure then, and were even less sure later. In fact, the debate would go on for months and would have an unbelievable number of shades of meaning — often depending on which lawyers were consulted. By the time the weary participants left 10 Downing, they had no firm plan as to what they and their countrymen should do.

Eden himself was undecided, although he went on record as intending to oppose Nasser in every way he could. But there were complications entwined in every possible solution. For example, if a lightning raid were made at Port Said in order to wrest the canal control back at that terminus, the other company offices would still be under Nasser's authority. And even if British assault troops were successful at the one spot, they would lack both support and replacement components necessary to sustain any occupation in the long run. Eden, as a former soldier and Military Cross winner, knew this. On the other hand, if Britain did nothing at all, Nasser would take the inaction as acquiescence to what had already been done.

In the heat of the moment, and because of his anger at the actions of the Egyptian president, Eden wanted to go into Port Said with all guns blazing, but he soon came face to face with a reality that he may have anticipated.

One of those called in that night was Earl Mountbatten of Burma, the First Sea Lord and, as it happened, the senior military man at the meeting. It was he who suggested that, as there happened to be British warships in Malta at the time, their relative proximity to Port Said could be advantageous. He also reminded Eden that there were over a thousand Royal Navy commandos stationed at Cyprus. The ships could take these troops to the north end of the canal, take control of it, and deprive Nasser of at least part of his gains. However, because of the aforementioned backup problems, Mountbatten's idea was deemed unwise. Instead, Eden asked him how long it would take to prepare for a full-fledged assault in Egypt, where adequate support and supply personnel would be available. When Mountbatten told the Prime Minister that it would take some weeks to assemble such an armada, Eden seems to have more or less expected such a reply. "He always had a shrewd suspicion that the forces, largely occupied in training, absorbing and replacing large numbers of conscript troops, standing guard for Nato [sic] and fighting colonial rebels were not well disposed to meet emergencies."[38] Mountbatten's assessment did not sit well with Eden. From that time on, they were not on the best of terms.

Shortly after the gathering at Downing Street, the American and French representatives reported to their respective governments on the substance of the meeting. A bit later that morning, Norman Robertson, Canadian High Commissioner to the United Kingdom, telegraphed Lester Pearson in Ottawa and filled the Minister of External Affairs in on the events of the previous night. His telegram was sent before 11:00 a.m. local time in London. While Robertson had not been at Eden's dinner, he had been briefed by the British Secretary of State for Commonwealth Relations, Lord Douglas Home, who had. In his message, Robertson mentioned the widespread consternation the canal nationalization was causing in Britain; in Home's words, the Government of the United Kingdom took "a very grave view" of the development. Then Robertson mentioned another factor that in the light of subsequent events was highly prescient: "I said that I assumed the Foreign Office would be considering the advantages and disadvantages of bringing this new situation to the notice of the Security Council."[39]

At that point, however, Eden resisted possible UN involvement because he felt the bureaucracy in New York would only hamper a reasonably quick reaction. As well, he was convinced that the Soviet Union would side with Egypt and veto any resolution that Britain might bring forward.

Eden met Parliament for the first time on what soon became known as the Suez Crisis at 11:00 a.m. on July 27, and called his first full

Cabinet meeting on the matter a mere fifteen minutes later. The general tone of the discussion resembled that of the previous night. In truth, there was still widespread uncertainty as to what to do — or at least, what to do first. As expected, Eden ran the show.

Across the nation, almost all of the major papers lined up solidly behind the Prime Minister, as did Hugh Gaitskell, the Leader of Her Majesty's Loyal Opposition. On the street at first, most Britons supported Eden and felt strongly that something had to be done, and soon. This general support would not last indefinitely, however, and in the weeks and months that followed, public opinion was badly split as to the government's actions. In London, for example, during research for this account, I talked to ordinary people who told me Eden's war was "insane." A long-term employee at the Imperial War Museum told me his own family was deeply divided over Suez. He said his father wanted to go to Egypt and smash Nasser, while his mother and uncles felt that since the canal was in Egypt, "Nasser might as well have it, as long as he kept it open." Others told me they were sure a third world war would break out over Suez. That, in fact, was the fear of many, albeit a little later on that summer.

By the end of the Cabinet meeting that Friday morning, some of the first tentative decisions had been made as to how to react to the nationalization. At the outset, formal contact would be made with the governments of the United States and France to arrange meetings with them in order to co-ordinate a response. To the Prime Minister, as to those around the Cabinet table, two things mattered most: the prestige of Britain and the oil supply. What Nasser had done was a slap in the face to Britain, and he could not be allowed to get away with it. The possibility of using force was discussed and not ruled out, whether France and the United States became involved or not. In this regard, an "agreement in principle to the use of force, even without assistance from the United States and France, reveals the prevailing assumption that, in that event, no opposition from the United States was expected, but at least tacit support."[40]

Canada was also kept abreast of developments. The next morning, Anthony Eden sent a message to Prime Minister Louis St. Laurent, in which he spelled out the situation as he saw it a little more than a day and a half after the fact. The note, marked "Secret," was both concise and blunt.

In it, Eden's controlled rage simmers just below the civility of the words. Of Nasser's actions, the British leader proclaimed: "We cannot allow him to get away with this act of expropriation and we must take a firm stand. If we do not, the oil supplies of the free world will be at his mercy and Commonwealth communications and trade will be gravely jeopardized."[41]

The letter also explained that representatives from Britain, the United States, and France would be meeting "with the object of concerting future action."[42] Such action would be taken so that the international operation and control of the canal could be maintained. If Egypt proved to be unreasonable, however, Eden threatened the use of force to achieve his aims. He concluded his note by promising to keep St. Laurent informed of the results of the upcoming meetings with the Americans and the French.

By the time Eden's message to St. Laurent was sent, Nasser had begun to adjust to the reality of Egypt being in control of the canal. He had long since concluded his nationalization address in Alexandria and had returned in triumph to Cairo by train. At the main railway station there, he was met by the thunderous applause of more than two hundred thousand delirious citizens. As he waved to them, they shouted, cheered, danced in the streets, and tossed flowers in his path. It took his driver an hour and a half to manoeuvre his Cadillac to the leader's headquarters. Normally, the trip took eight minutes at most.

Nasser went to his office window, looked out over the vast crowd below, and acknowledged their applause. He had stood up to the "outsiders" who were forever intent on ruling his country and who wanted to exploit it for their own ends. He mentioned the shock waves that even then were reverberating through Britain, France, the United States, and indeed all the Western nations.

And then he had an ominous message for them all: "I strongly warn the imperialist countries that their evil games will be the reason for disturbing free navigation in the Suez Canal."[43] He stressed that the canal should remain open and that navigation through it should continue uninterrupted. However, it would be up to the West — Britain and France in particular — to see that ships would continue to pass through the waterway. In other words, if the canal became blocked, they and not Egypt would be to blame.

To a large degree, Gamal Nasser's warning had become Lester Pearson's worst fear. For the next few frantic months, his every word and deed as a public figure would be focused on keeping the canal open and counteracting whatever came about that threatened to close it. He began the quest with a heavy heart.

CHAPTER FIVE

Hitler on the Nile

BECAUSE OF HIS TAKEOVER of the Suez Canal, Gamal Nasser became the new Hitler in many quarters of both Britain and France, and to a lesser extent elsewhere. The London *Daily Mail* newspaper called him "Hitler on the Nile" shortly after the nationalization. His book *The Philosophy of the Revolution* was compared to Hitler's *Mein Kampf*, and it suddenly became required reading in Western embassies. When it was first published in 1955, however, it was looked upon with admiration. American syndicated columnist Dorothy Thompson wrote an introduction in which she praised Nasser, lauded what he wrote, and called his book "remarkable for the painful, humble, self-searching and self-analysis that the leader of the Egyptian revolution makes of himself and — even more courageously — of his country and its people."[44]

But she wrote these words before the canal takeover. Now that the nationalization had been carried out, politicians of every stripe denounced the book and its author every time they got the chance. French Premier Guy Mollet looked upon Nasser as an Arab Hitler who was actively plotting against the West. Colonel Louis Mangin, an aide to French Defence Minister Maurice Bourges-Maunoury, "caused descent in France's declining relations with Egypt by openly referring to Nasser as Hitler."[45] Gradually, most newspapers in the U.K. swung around to the *Daily Mail* perspective, and with them, a great many readers as well.

As far as Anthony Eden was concerned, Nasser's actions reminded the Prime Minister of earlier times when his nation and the world were slow to react to Nazi aggression. Such a viewpoint was particularly acute for

Eden, as a former diplomat and military man. He had become determined to ensure that another Hitler would never arise. For that reason, he closely aligned himself with the French point of view, and actively sought confirmation for his feelings from the Americans as well. Indeed, even President Eisenhower and John Foster Dulles seemed to share similar fears. When an American senator asked Dulles if possibly getting rid of Nasser might bring an even less desirable leader on the Nile, Dulles mentioned the "Hitlerite" personality of Nasser, and added that he was "the worst so far."[46]

In a briefing to senior members of both the Senate and the House of Representatives, President Dwight Eisenhower also evoked the spectre of the Nazi dictator when he said Nasser's actions were "much like Hitler's in *Mein Kampf*, a book no one believed."[47] Yet Hitler acted on what he had written, and it seemed Nasser had as well.

But were his actions legal?

The subject came up initially at the after-dinner meeting at 10 Downing, and it would do so again and again in the days that followed. Eden always believed Nasser's actions were illegal and a flagrant breach of international convention. He nonetheless felt he had to go through the charade of at least getting professional advice concerning the question. To that end, experts in the legal department of the Foreign Office were asked to look into the move on the canal and then come back and render their opinion. They did as directed and examined what Nasser had done from all possible angles. They looked at everything, from long forgotten statutes to dusty archival opinions to international points of view and related precedents. They examined the fine print in the 1888 Convention of Constantinople and the working papers that supported it. They consulted known experts in the field of international and maritime law. They sought the advice of authorities in other countries, and they finally arrived at a conclusion — a conclusion that Eden ridiculed and rejected out of hand.

A lawyer from the Foreign Office had to deliver the word. The poor unfortunate went to Eden's office at mid-morning of July 27, shortly before the Prime Minister was to leave for Westminster. The man informed Eden that "unless Nasser closed the canal to shipping — which he was not proposing to do — the nationalization was quite legal."[48] The Prime Minister's reaction was extreme. "Eden took the report, read it through, then tore it into pieces and flung it in the lawyer's face."[49] As the barrister beat a hasty retreat, the Prime Minister bellowed, "I don't care whether it's legal or not, I'm not going to let him get away with it."[50]

It would not be the last time this volatile temper was on display. But Eden was not alone in his views on the illegality of what Nasser had done. Even though he seemed to waffle in his opinion, Harold Macmillan also felt that Nasser had broken the law. In a discussion of Dulles's role in the Aswan Dam affair, which he called "a diplomatic error" on the part of the American, Macmillan referred to the consequences of Nasser's "illegal action."[51] U.K. Foreign Minister Selwyn Lloyd was of the same opinion. He voiced this point of view at the 10 Downing Street meeting and said it publicly on several occasions, one of which was in a speech he made at the United Nations Security Council in New York on October 5, 1956. Later, in his own self-justifying memoir about Suez, he was even more blunt: "I had discussed with my advisers in the Foreign Office the legality of Nasser's actions in international law. We had little doubt about the illegality of his action."[52] Lloyd's words must be read with a measure of skepticism, however, because he was probably talking to the same Foreign Office experts who gave the opposite view to Eden.

And yet, Lloyd had no intention of backing down. He claimed several of his colleagues shared his opinion — and they probably did — including Robert Menzies, Prime Minister of Australia, and Clifton Webb, a former Attorney General of New Zealand.

But here in Canada, Lloyd's viewpoint was not supported and, by implication, neither was Eden's. On July 27, Lester Pearson was asked by Ottawa reporters for his reaction to what Nasser had done and to what the U.K. and France might do in response. In reply, the Minister urged caution in whatever action might be taken. He pointed out to the press that Canada was concerned about any closure of the canal, particularly because it was an international waterway. He added that Canada had neither ownership of nor dealings with the Suez Canal Company as such.

The following day, Pearson cabled a lengthy top-secret message to Norman Robertson, Canadian High Commissioner in London. In it, Pearson mentioned his remarks to the Ottawa media and then spelled out his own feelings about what the President of Egypt had done. "It would appear," he wrote, "that there has been no technical violation of the Constantinople Convention so long as the Egyptians do not interfere with shipping through the canal."[53]

Pearson then turned to Eden's earlier note and the strident tone he was adopting with regard to the nationalization. In this area, Pearson came close to predicting how the Americans might react. "I am deeply concerned," he told Robertson, "at the implications of some parts of Eden's message; especially as I doubt very much whether he will receive strong support from Washington in the firm line he proposes to follow."[54]

His foresight was prophetic.

The reaction of the Americans was of interest, not only to Canada, Britain, and France, but to other countries as well, including Egypt. A long-time confidant and friend of Nasser's later summarized Egyptian feelings when he wrote, "It was not clear what line the Americans were going to take. In some respects they seemed as hostile as the British and French." He added, however, that "there seemed a hope that it might be possible to separate them from their partners." For that reason, he said, "Nasser repeated several times that nationalization of the canal ... was not intended as a rebuff to America."[55]

As expected, the Chinese and the Russians supported Egypt. The Soviet news agency TASS, on July 29, claimed that President Nasser's move had been made to help his people. In the same breath, however, Moscow cautioned Britain and France against resorting to war over the matter. They realized that if the nationalization led to military conflict, they too could be embroiled in it. So, for that matter, did the United States.

It was Dwight Eisenhower who was largely responsible for the next development in the crisis. John Foster Dulles was in South America when the situation broke, so Eisenhower immediately dispatched a ranking State Department official to a series of tripartite talks in London. These discussions would include Britain, France, and the United States and were designed to formulate some kind of mutually acceptable response to Nasser's move. The representative was a man named Robert Murphy, whose main role, it seems, was to find out what was going on and to ensure that cooler heads prevailed as long as possible. In all likelihood, Eisenhower sent Murphy only because the President felt his country needed to be represented in whatever moves were made while giving Dulles the time to return and clarify the American position. In effect, that is what happened. However, before Murphy could reach his destination, some important peripheral decisions were made.

On July 28, the Treasury in Britain moved to freeze all Egyptian Suez Canal Company assets in the U.K. The next day, France did the same thing, as did the U.S. two days after that. Britain also decreed that from July 30, it would be illegal for any firm in that country to sell arms to the Egyptians.

As soon as Murphy arrived, and then, shortly afterwards, Dulles as well, the talks involving the three powers got underway, continuing until August 2. To a degree they were inconclusive, but they did serve as a kind of stop-gap measure. Their main accomplishment was an agreement that Egypt's actions could be deemed a threat to the continued operation of the canal. Representatives at the discussions then concurred that further talks were necessary. By this time, "some 20,000 British Army reservists were called up, and naval, military and air reinforcements were despatched to the eastern Mediterranean."[56] Even to the casual observer, it was obvious that Britain was on the verge of war.

Eden was quickly becoming obsessed by Nasser, which threatened to make the situation even graver than it appeared. For example, he sent President Eisenhower "a very secret message that he had decided that the only way to break Nasser would be to resort to force without delay and without attempting to negotiate."[57] And while Eden wanted to remove Nasser as leader of Egypt, he nevertheless seems to have given little thought to who might replace him. He just wanted Nasser out.

In Washington, Eisenhower recoiled from the idea of going to war over the canal. For that reason, he strongly supported his Secretary of State in all attempts to ameliorate something that was rapidly spinning out of control. As soon as Dulles got back to his office, he was presented with the misgivings of his president and urged to come up with a solution that would offer at least a cooling-off period before there was any resort to arms.

Dulles acted with dispatch. Largely through his efforts and his sometimes less than subtle persuasion, Britain, France, and a host of other nations agreed to participate in an international conference that would examine the Suez Canal, its operation, and its value to those nations that used it. The conference delegates would also look at what Nasser had done and decide in concert how to react. Those involved convened at the stately Lancaster House in London at 10:00 a.m. on Thursday, August 16. Representatives from twenty-two countries were there, among them the top sixteen users of the canal. Egypt was invited but did not attend. As only an occasional user of the canal, Canada was not invited.

As usual with such gatherings, there were lots of speeches, plenty of politicking, and even more backroom negotiation. Delegates assembled that first morning to hear Dulles and then broke into committees and evaluated everything he and others had proposed. But it was Dulles's plan that carried the day, and it was his proposal that ended up being voted on as the sessions concluded.

Dulles suggested that an international board be appointed to actually operate the canal. The specific makeup of such a board would be negotiated, and the nations most affected would have at least tacit input into the way the waterway worked. In order to soothe Egyptian passions, Dulles suggested that that country be given more of the revenues accruing from canal usage and that the shareholders of the Suez Canal Company be compensated for any losses they had suffered.

As might be expected, international response to the plan differed, with a handful of nations either remaining neutral in their assessment or supporting Egypt. The majority of those present, however, backed Dulles. And it was Dulles, the bull-in-the-china-shop American diplomat, who got most of the accolades over what had been accomplished.

And what was that? If Britain and France were kept at the table talking, neither was dropping bombs. The more time elapsed, the more their rhetoric subsided. They had been chided by other nations and they knew it. A major American magazine declared, in describing the positive effects, "Under the combined barrages of so many critics, the British and French governments began to temper their words."[58] The positive perception also spilled out onto the streets of Britain. As time passed, more and more of the people, the newspapers, and the politicians declared themselves less interested in resorting to the war so many had wanted immediately after the nationalization.

In Cairo, the feeling was remarkable similar, but for a totally different reason. As a Nasser senior adviser said, his country wanted the talks in London to continue as long as possible because "Nasser wanted to gain time. [He] was working on world public opinion,"[59] and he wanted to bring the world to his side. Nasser, the politician, knew that the more any firm decision on a long-term solution to the canal crisis could be put off, the more anti-Egyptian feelings would be tempered. Reaction to major news events declines as newspaper headlines fade.

Here in Canada, the federal Cabinet met on August 29, and the Suez question was paramount in the discussions. Because both the United States and Britain had asked Canada for support of the Lancaster House conclusions, the matter was raised by Lester Pearson, debated on at length, and given concurrence. The extract from Cabinet Conclusions of the day affirmed "that Canada supported the plan of the majority of the London Conference … as a satisfactory basis for a solution to the problem."[60]

But the matter had not been laid to rest. In Britain and France, war preparations continued even as the diplomats postured.

CHAPTER SIX

The Problem of Egypt

AT 7:20 P.M. ON WEDNESDAY, AUGUST 1, 1956, the Chiefs of Staff of the British Armed Forces met with Anthony Eden and his Cabinet. During that meeting, the military leaders unveiled a set of plans entitled *Action Against Egypt*. The presentation was the first major response to the Suez Canal nationalization, and because Eden and most of those around him were in favour of a quick strike against Nasser, what they heard that evening must have been disappointing. In essence, the Chiefs said they were unprepared for war at that time.

They drew particular attention to the need to train paratroops, who would be central to any attack on Egypt and on the Canal Zone specifically. This lack of readiness came about because in the previous years, airborne troops had been involved in putting down guerrilla operations on the island of Cyprus. In that action, little if any jumping had been necessary. Furthermore, much military planning since the end of the Second World War had been of a traditional nature, involving operations similar to the assault on the Germans in Normandy twelve years earlier. So even though "the employment of paratroopers for an action against the Suez Canal had been contemplated, the Chiefs of Staff expressed their preference for a maritime blockade, possibly combined with air operations."[61]

This was just the type of thing Eden did not want to hear. Like George W. Bush in later years, who was determined to have his war in Iraq no matter what, Anthony Eden had his mind set on attacking Egypt and eliminating Nasser right away, despite any cautionary advice he received.

It was therefore in the face of such a state of indecision that the armed forces were told to prepare some kind of response to Nasser, and sooner rather than later. Eden did not want the British public to fault him for doing nothing. Nor did he like being judged against the way his immediate predecessor might have acted. Winston Churchill, with his "we shall fight on the beaches" kind of rhetoric, had mobilized his nation in a way Eden never could. Churchill had acted; Eden believed he would be criticized if he did not.

With that in mind, he pressed the Chiefs to do what they could against Nasser now, even with under-trained personnel, a lack of proper equipment (such as landing craft), and a limited number of air bases within striking distance of Egypt. In the days that followed, the military leaders did the best they could. The preparations were not made under blanket secrecy, because it was commonly assumed that Britain would respond to Nasser. As well, as far as Eden was concerned, if the general populace saw war preparations being made, it would demonstrate that he was exercising leadership. He did consult with Churchill and listened to the great man's advice, but he knew that whatever happened in Egypt, good or bad, was his responsibility. If standing up to Nasser was successful, he would be praised; if the response to the nationalization was inadequate, he knew he would be held accountable.

In an act reminiscent of Churchill's dramatic exhortations in time of war, Eden asked for and received permission to use the airwaves to get his message across. Whether he brought many of the undecided around to his point of view was debatable. Unfortunately, his words, intended to be stirring, were not particularly memorable. Although the Egyptian President's action may not have been catastrophic, Eden seemed to believe that it was. He told his countrymen that what Nasser had done was "a matter of life and death," and then continued, "Why is it so terrible to nationalize a company? It was done here. That is perfectly true, but it was done ... to our own British industry. Colonel Nasser's action is entirely different. He has taken over the international company without consultation and without consent."[62]

He then turned to Nasser's promise not to interfere with canal shipping. He told his people that Nasser's words were unreliable and that he could not be trusted. He added that Britain's quarrel was not with Egypt, or even with the Arab world. It was with Nasser, who, Eden feared, would close the canal just as quickly as he had taken it over. For that reason, even though he hoped the situation could be worked out by consultation and international diplomacy, he feared it could not. Of the nationalization itself, Eden stressed, "We cannot agree that an act of plunder which threatens the livelihood of many nations shall be allowed to succeed."[63] In so saying, the Prime Minister, to a degree, painted himself into a corner. He intended to mobilize his nation and send its sons and daughters into harm's way because Nasser could not be trusted, despite whatever international agreement might be in place to supervise Suez.

As each day passed, more and more military call-ups were made, and more reservists who thought they were through saluting found themselves back in uniform. They did some marching, were handed a rifle, and were told they were going to sea. In due course, they boarded ships in places like Portsmouth and steamed south across the Bay of Biscay to Gibraltar and then on towards the eastern Mediterranean.

While the French were upset at Nasser because of the canal nationalization, they also had another, equally strong reason to be angry with him. West of Egypt and occupying a vast swath of North Africa was French Algeria. From 1879, the territory had been under civil rule as part of France. During the Second World War it fell under Vichy control for a time, but afterwards had been occupied by the Allies. By 1954, however, nationalist factions within the area were carrying out guerrilla insurrections and demanding independence from France, activities that were ongoing in 1956. (They eventually got their wish in 1962.) In Paris, the government of the day blamed Gamal Nasser for fomenting this rebellion. The feeling in France was that if they could deal with him about the canal problem, they might be able to solve their Algerian difficulties at the same time. Thus, the idea of toppling Nasser became a rather welcome one. Doing so would also save France a lot of money. For some time, the cost of dealing with the Algerian insurrection had been a severe drain on the treasury of France. And to make matters worse, the Algerian Front de Liberation Nationale was gaining strength each day. This organization was a huge thorn in the side of France, and there was little doubt that Egypt, and specifically Nasser, was sympathetic to its aims.

There was also a third country that had ongoing difficulties with Egypt in general and with its ruler in particular. Since the day of its inception, Israel had never been able to relax as long as Egypt did not accept its existence. And while Egypt had been beaten in every skirmish the two had had, the anti-Israeli rhetoric and harassment had continued. For that reason, David Ben Gurion and the other power figures in the Jewish state could never lower their guard. In such a climate of distrust, if not outright hatred, it was no wonder Israel sought to end border problems once and for all. Israel had "anticipated a war with Egypt before the summer [of 1956] and had started preparations for a pre-emptive strike, aimed at ending the fedayeen attacks, safeguarding its harbour at Eilat, and diminishing the strength of the Egyptian army."[64] The port town of Eilat, or Elat, would become Israel's leading oil port. Because of its location at the head of the Gulf of Aqaba, near Egypt, Jordan, and Saudi Arabia, it was especially important to Israel.

It was in such a tense situation that the leading military figures for the looming war were installed. As Britain felt it had the most to gain — or lose — by getting rid of Nasser and securing the Suez, the British appointed a respected soldier named Charles Keightley as commander-in-chief to head a combined operation with France against Egypt as soon as the time was right. Serving under Keightley was General Hugh Stockwell, who was named task force commander for the British and French ground forces. The senior French officer during the Suez Crisis was General Andre Beaufre, deputy to Stockwell. These two men had illustrious military backgrounds, and from all accounts they worked well together and accomplished as much as they could of what they were directed to do. In only one instance did they make what might be called a serious error in judgment, but that would not occur until later. It is safe to say that the appointments were praiseworthy.

THE MAJOR DECISION made at the close of the twenty-two-country London conference on August 23 was that an international advisory board be put in place to operate the Suez Canal. Australian Prime Minister Robert Menzies was directed to lead a delegation to Cairo to present the suggestion to Nasser and get his reaction to it. The mission might have been laudable, but the wrong man was picked to head it.

Robert Menzies was an admirer of John Foster Dulles, seeing him as a kind of mentor who rarely made a misstep. He felt that Dulles feared nothing and that in his public performance had been proven right more often than proven wrong. Like Dulles, Menzies was a hothead, and when crossed he could be just as temperamental as the powerful American statesman. For that reason, at a time when a delicate political touch might have brought about some success, Menzies' way of dealing with Nasser greatly irritated the Egyptian. Menzies and those with him were wasting their time in Cairo.

Menzies was also a staunch ally and friend of Anthony Eden. He strongly backed the British leader's approach to Suez, and while he was in London for the conference he said so in a television address that Eden urged him to make. In the broadcast, Eden thought the Australian Leader spoke "admirably."[65]

But in Cairo all Menzies' good intentions broke down — though it is doubtful if the mission would have succeeded in any event. Even before the Australian leader arrived in Egypt, Nasser and his advisers pretty well knew what to expect. "The reports that reached Cairo spoke of Menzies as being an extremely tough character who was bringing with him an ultimatum which would amount to a knockout blow for Nasser,"[66] wrote one of the Egyptian President's closest confidants. The same writer claimed that, after the two statesmen met for the first of four times, Nasser referred to Menzies as an "Australian mule."[67]

And Menzies' opinion of the Egyptian leader was just as caustic. "I was told that Nasser was a man of great personal charm," Menzies wrote in a letter to Eden a week or so later. "That is not so. He is in some ways quite a likeable fellow but ... he is rather *gauche*, with some irritating mannerisms, such as rolling his eyes to the ceiling when he is talking to you and producing a quick, quite evanescent grin when he can think of nothing else to do. I would say that he was a man of considerable but immature intelligence."[68] No wonder Menzies failed.

In Ottawa, Lester Pearson reflected in a rather gentle way on the results of the mission when he wrote, "Mr. Menzies was not exactly the kind of man likely to create the best impression on Nasser."[69]

While the international bickering over who would control Suez Canal operations continued, a much more fundamental concern was arising at the waterway itself. In his nationalization speech, Nasser had directed that the canal was to remain open and passage through it was to continue without interruption or harassment. In a more controversial directive at the time, he also ordered all canal employees to remain at their workstations. They did so, and tanker traffic remained fairly constant.

But the two-hundred-plus Suez pilots who took command of vessels within the canal itself were, for the most part, foreign nationals. Most of them were either French or British, with no more than forty or so Egyptians. Those ratios had been in place for some time.

These individuals boarded the ships transiting the canal and in effect became temporary captains. The pilot had to navigate the often problematic waterway and deal with shifting wind, restricted space, occasionally blowing sand, and sometimes fog so thick the view from the bridge barely extended to the ship's bow. Because of the narrowness of the canal itself, any breakdown, grounding, or accident could block passage for days. For all of those reasons, both the British and the French had always refused to expand the Egyptian pilot corps. The feeling at the time, tinged with a smug kind of racism, was that the Egyptians were just not up to the job.

As one historian put it: "The European pilots … exaggerated the difficulties of the job in order to assert their own uniqueness and importance."[70] The same writer also pointed out that "the world at large … held the Egyptians in contempt, overlooking the fact that for 5,000 years they had been taking ships under sail up and down the shifting course of the Nile, which required more technical virtuosity than piloting an engine-driven ship through a current-less canal."[71] Even though Nasser had forbidden the foreign pilots to leave their posts, he was quite aware of the fact that some wanted to do so, despite whatever dangers or difficulties they might face. The Anglo-French owners of the Suez Canal Company told their employees that if they did not resign, they would forfeit whatever pensions they might expect. On the other hand, the new Egyptian bosses warned them that if they did quit, they would never be allowed to pilot a ship in Egyptian waters again. In spite of, or because of, their dilemma, over a period of weeks most of the foreigners got out.

As soon as they left, however, nationals from elsewhere came on stream.

The Egyptians immediately began to not only recruit more of their own, but also advertise around the world for replacement pilots. Canadian papers carried some of these ads, but the response from here, if any, is unknown. Some Americans signed on, as did many Russians, a number of Germans, and a smattering of recruits from other countries. The new pay scale was quite generous, and that was a key factor in the response from abroad. The Egyptian pilots that were already working had their hours extended, their expertise put to good use, and their contribution to the nation acknowledged. Nasser pinned medals of merit on those who helped most; they had performed beyond all expectations. In the first month under the new regime, more ships were taken through the waterway than in the month prior to the nationalization. In his public statements about Suez, Nasser made sure the world knew this.

So it was that, temporarily, the Suez situation cooled slightly. Anthony Eden remained as determined as ever to oust Nasser, and England and France were even more keen to go to war. Ironically, as the ships moved unhampered through the canal, war preparations to ensure such movement expanded. At the same time, the American who created the plan to prevent war went to his cottage for a much-needed break from work. His vacation spot was called Duck Island, a clump of rock, bush, and beach he had owned for many years in Lake Ontario, near Kingston. Dulles loved to spend time there, and did so as often as he could. He found the place invigorating, this time perhaps more so than on other occasions. After his cottage weekend, as Anthony Eden pointed out, Dulles arrived back in Washington "with some fresh thoughts."[72]

Even though Dulles's thoughts might not have been either new or particularly fresh, they did serve their purpose — at least for a time. Ships might have been moving through Suez, but the threat of a third world war over the canal was as great as ever. For that reason, anything that Dulles proposed was not only important, it was vital.

CHAPTER SEVEN

Anglo-French Decisions

BY THE TIME AMERICAN SECRETARY OF STATE John Foster Dulles got back to Washington after his weekend in Canada, he had pretty well decided what he intended to do in order to circumvent or at least delay a war. Already the British and French had made rapid progress in military preparations, and more and more of their troops were pouring into various staging grounds, particularly in Cyprus. Plans had initially been drawn up for an attack on the Egyptian port city of Alexandria, but this had since been changed to Port Said. Britain still wanted American approval in whatever way possible, but this did not seem to be forthcoming. Dulles stepped into the hiatus.

While at his cottage, he had gone over in his own mind an idea he had already mentioned in passing to Anthony Eden. This was for some kind of formal organization that would be beneficial to the operations of the Suez Canal. Eden had guessed, rightly as it turned out, that Nasser would have nothing to do with the Menzies proposals. A somewhat similar but more equitable plan might have more appeal, not necessarily in Cairo, but in the capitals of the nations whose ships used Suez. Dulles probably knew his second plan would also fail, but it did gain time. The longer war could be put off, the smaller the chances that it would happen at all. At least, that was his hope.

The Dulles Plan, as British Foreign Secretary Selwyn Lloyd described it, would mean that "the users of the canal should bind themselves together, hire the pilots, manage the technical features of the canal, organize the pattern of navigation and collect the dues from the ships of member countries."[73] Lloyd liked the idea, but his French counterpart, Christain Pineau, did not. This was because "French policy-makers [including Pineau] mistrusted American intentions and considered the users' association as an attempt to postpone force indefinitely."[74] And that was exactly what it was. On Lloyd's insistence, the French reluctantly agreed that the Dulles Plan should at least be considered. For that reason a second conference about Suez came to be.

Plans for the gathering took form rather quickly. Messages to all the major canal users went out, and one by one, they agreed. They dispatched representatives to London, where the meetings were to be held, and none of them seemed to oppose the American initiative. Perhaps they just did not want to alienate Dulles. He was certainly the most powerful Secretary of State ever, and all of them knew it. They did his bidding, and while they may have liked his proposals, they did not like him. That included many Canadians who dealt with him on occasion.

In an interview for another book some years ago, I asked Canadian political scientist and diplomat Doctor G.P. de T. Glazebrook about Dulles. Glazebrook worked in the Department of External Affairs and in the course of his duties had dealings with Dulles. None were pleasant, and Glazebrook visibly recoiled when I mentioned Dulles's name. "He was a pompous know-it-all," Glazebrook recalled, "and whatever you did for him was never good enough. I ended up disliking the man intensely." In his book *The Presidents and the Prime Ministers*, author Lawrence Martin also mentions the Dulles-Glazebrook connection. "To George Glazebrook, he [Dulles] was the prototype American power-pusher that Canadians disliked most, a bull-headed autocrat."[75]

Former Canadian national news announcer Knowlton Nash shared the same point of view and called Dulles "righteous, rigid, and arrogant … a man utterly lacking in humour or grace."[76] Anthony Eden did not get too close to the American politician either, but for a completely different reason. "Eden was repelled by Dulles's fierce halitosis and tended to keep his distance."[77] Such are the foibles of the great men of history.

THE SECOND CONFERENCE of the Suez Crisis opened in London on the morning of September 19. Again, the setting was Lancaster House, and

British Foreign Secretary Selwyn Lloyd chaired the affair. Dulles addressed the representatives of the eighteen nations gathered there, and on the afternoon of the first day he presented his proposal. The result of the deliberations was the formation of something called the Suez Canal Users' Association, or SCUA. It had little or no power and was virtually ignored from the moment of its inception. Since Suez, historians have spent more time laughing at the first acronym for the association, which meant "testicle" in Portuguese, than they have assessing its merits. Needless to say, the first name was set aside. As expected, Nasser denounced the results anyway.

Two other major developments occurred around this time. The first involved France and Britain; the second, France and Israel.

In the first, Anthony Eden and Guy Mollet, the prime minister of France, decided to submit the Suez problem to the Security Council of the United Nations in New York. They had long hesitated to do so, particularly because they knew the Soviet Union would veto virtually all proposals pertaining to the canal that had French or British backing. In fact, Dulles had argued that any submission to the Security Council would go nowhere. After all, no one had proven that Nasser had broken any law, so the Russians would be sure to exploit that point of view. Furthermore, the U.S.S.R. was intent on embarrassing Britain and the United States because the Soviet toehold in the Middle East had been strengthened by their offer to finance and build Nasser's dam.

So why did Eden and Mollet suddenly decide to go to the UN now? Because of pressure. Both had been urged by ever-larger factions within their own countries to get the UN involved. As well, world opinion at the time favoured some kind of negotiated end to the nationalization debacle. Talk was better than war, and certainly better than war over something that might have been legal in the first place. In Britain, the Labour Opposition had long since backed away from its early outrage over what Nasser had done. Hugh Gaitskell might have been vociferous in supporting Eden on the night the nationalization was announced, but since that critical evening, his anger had subsided markedly. Now it became more and more clear that Eden could not get agreement from all sides, no matter what he did. He would have been criticized whether he went to the UN or not.

By going to the Security Council, he also alienated Dulles, but even expecting that, he seems to have deliberately decided to leave the belligerent American out of the loop insofar as Suez was concerned. He and Mollet laid their case before the Security Council, and the flabbergasted Secretary of State found out about it after it happened. From that time on, France and Britain acted first and told the Americans afterwards — particularly on a matter that was far more sinister than recourse to the Security Council, a matter that Anthony Eden would deny ever happened. In fact, he ultimately took his denial to his grave. It involved collusion with Israel over Suez.

For some time during the summer of 1956, French politicians had been talking to their Israeli counterparts about the Suez question in general and, of more importance to the Jewish state, about Egypt's belligerence as exemplified by the continued raids of the fedayeen along the Egyptian-Israeli border. Israel regarded such incursions as threats to its existence and responded to them with a vengeance that was both swift and harsh. While neither side was without blame, the raids and reprisals continued and even escalated in their severity. It was into this mix that Israel appealed to France for more help: more arms, more fighter planes, and more advanced technology in order to counter Nasser's initiatives.

And France listened — but for reasons that were also in its own interest.

The French came to the realization that if they helped Israel in its never-ending problems with Egypt, then perhaps they could use Israel in some kind of scheme that would help them deal with Nasser on both the canal question and Algeria. Initially, Britain was not a party to any French-Israeli talks, and whether Selwyn Lloyd ever guessed that they were taking place at all is uncertain. Needless to say, the early French-Israeli consultations were held in the utmost secrecy. However, once Britain became a rather reluctant third party, the shroud of silence was almost impenetrable.

Prime Minister Guy Mollet, Foreign Minister Christian Pineau, and senior military officials in France began to meet with high-level Israeli representatives to discuss the security of the Jewish state and to brainstorm ways in which that security could be enhanced. The talks went well, and France sold Mystère fighter jets to Israel, concealing from the world the numbers sold. Other equipment was provided as well. France hoped Israel would use these arms against Egypt, not just to get rid of the fedayeen problem but to topple Nasser as well. To France, the Algerian situation was becoming more critical by the day.

The next development originated in France. Because the French and the British were already working together in the buildup to a probable attack on Egypt, the French decided to confide in the British about the bilateral discussions with Israel. The thought was that "an Israeli attack on Egypt would offer an opportunity for France and Great Britain to intervene in the Canal Zone."[78] While both Eden and Mollet wanted to attack Egypt and topple Nasser, they were very much aware of the opposition to the move, both within their own countries and elsewhere. So while "the French put the issue to the British as a problem of contingency planning,"[79] Eden was extremely worried about possible repercussions resulting from a contrived arrangement for war. Nevertheless, that is what came to pass.

The proposed collusion with the Israelis only increased the pressure Eden was under during those days in September. He was frustrated because invasion preparations were taking so long. He was finding it harder and harder to keep his parliamentary caucus on side. He had to deal with anti-war sentiment that was building across the land. He was so annoyed at Dulles that he not only ceased confiding in him, he did all he could to gain invasion support — at least tacitly — from Dwight Eisenhower. But at no time did the American president advise him to go to war.

Eden also read the papers, and what they said about him was often not good. He was accused of being weak, of vacillating, of being out of touch, of showing poor leadership, and of refusing to listen to advice that was not in accordance with his own point of view. The press often compared him to Churchill, and almost never favourably. And, sadly, "Eden was not tough; he had not been hardened by criticism. For too long, he had been the 'Golden Boy' of the Conservative Party ... the 'Crown Prince' who basked in Churchill's admiration."[80] But not anymore. And that was not all.

Anthony Eden was a sick man.

Three years earlier, shortly before the coronation of Queen Elizabeth on June 2, 1953, Eden became seriously ill with gallbladder trouble. He was operated on in Britain at first, and later in the United States as well. The early operations were not successful, and the ones that followed were only partially effective. "In total, he had nine major internal operations"[81] for the original ailment, and then more for the surgical complications that occurred when the doctors were trying to correct it. One medical procedure lasted more than eight hours and was so serious that the patient was accorded only a fifty-fifty chance of recovery. He did recover, but from then on was rarely well. The problem came to a head at the worst possible time: when Eden was doing his best to contain the whirlwind the Suez affair brought to his door. He was in constant pain; his sleep, when it came, was of short duration and was disturbed. He became incensed at small things, and he often took his frustrations out on those who worked closest to him. Sometimes, an apparently innocuous comment would lead to yet another explosion. Historian Captain B.H. Liddell Hart experienced an Eden temper tantrum first-hand.

Liddell Hart was a well-known and highly respected military expert who had been asked to draw up a set of plans for an attack on Egypt. He did so — several times. Eden read each of the drafts, tore it apart, and angrily returned it for additional work. When the fourth rejection landed back on his desk, an exasperated Liddell Hart had had enough. Instead of drawing up a fifth version, he went back to his first submission, slipped it into a packet, and had it hand-delivered to Eden's office.

This time, Eden loved the plan, but instead of thanking the historian for a job well done, the Prime Minister ordered the man to 10 Downing. In due course, the tall, slim, impeccably dressed expert was ushered into Eden's office. Once there, he was on the receiving end of a prime-ministerial tirade.

As Liddell Hart listened in surprised and shocked silence, Eden ranted at length about how hard it was to run the country at a time of crisis. He was dealing with life and death situations every day, he fumed, but in return got unsatisfactory performance from those entrusted with carrying out his wishes. He then harangued his visitor for having taken five attempts to get the requested plan right, when it should have been done properly the first time.

At this point, the historian probably should have held his tongue, but the pointed criticism and the way it was delivered was demeaning. In attempting to defend himself, Liddell Hart pointed out to Eden that the now-satisfactory plan was actually the first one that had been submitted.

Hearing this, Eden became visibly enraged: his face went scarlet, and he lost control. Without saying a word, he reached across his desk, grabbed the bottle of ink that was on it, and hurled it across the room, right at Liddell Hart. His aim was accurate. Almost immediately, the cream-coloured summer suit that the historian was wearing was not quite what it had been.

For a few seconds, neither man spoke. Then "Liddell Hart looked down at the sickly blue stains spreading across his immaculate linen suiting, uncoiled himself, picked up a government-issue wastepaper basket, and jammed it over the prime minister's head before slowly walking out of the room."[82]

The encounter was over — but accounts of the incident circulated for years.

Prime Minister Anthony Eden continued to ignore the best medical advice he had. He insisted on working, consuming painkillers, and going without rest — all the while making decisions that were critical to the future of his country and the world.

CHAPTER EIGHT

A Case of Collusion

THE FRENCH, ISRAELI, AND BRITISH COLLUSION came to a climax in the third week of October 1956. By that time, all three countries had committed themselves to a concerted action that became an ill-concealed international hoax, in spite of all the secrecy that led up to it. Travels were not publicized, trips were made under assumed names, and journeys were taken where the ultimate destination was not revealed to even the closest associates of the people involved. Through all the clandestine meetings, there was an air of mistrust in every one of the participants. In fact, this mistrust was so palpable at times, it is a wonder the scheme ended up working at all — or at least working as well as it did.

The main architect of the endeavour was French General Maurice Challe, deputy to the French Chief of the General Staff, who "proposed the intervention of France and Great Britain to safeguard the Suez Canal in case of an Israeli attack on Egypt."[83] This was a reasonably concise explanation for so many of the actions that followed. What the perpetrators of the Challe plan did not want to admit to the world was that the whole affair was a set piece. Israel would attack Egypt at an agreed time, then France and Britain would rush in, not to aid Egypt, of course, but to "save" the canal. Then the three nations involved would deny that the scenario was pre-arranged.

Precise plans for the collusion were made at Sevres, France, at a beautiful old mansion on the fringes of Paris. The building had earlier played a role as a resistance base during the Second World War, so it was rather appropriate that it would now be the location where more secret plans were made. The place was chosen because it was out of the way, little known, and, within the context of its surroundings, largely innocuous. The first meetings there were between the French and the Israelis. Shortly thereafter, British representatives came as well. While Eden reluctantly approved of the plan and then urged those closest to him to support it, he never actually went to Sevres himself. He had others who acted for him there.

The senior representatives of the countries involved were Guy Mollet and Christian Pineau of France, David Ben Gurion and Moshe Dayan of Israel, and Selwyn Lloyd and, substituting for him at the final Sevres meeting, Sir Patrick Dean of the British Foreign Office. All of these participants kept their journeys to Sevres as low-key as possible. French representatives went in their own cars, while the Israeli and the British representatives flew into the small military airport at Villacoublay, not far from Sevres. They were met there and then taken in unmarked vehicles to the conference centre.

The climate at the gathering was tense from the outset, never more so than when Ben Gurion said that he wanted to postpone action for a short time and that he envisioned a much larger military campaign that would ultimately involve other Middle Eastern countries. In Ben Gurion's vision, for example, was the partitioning of Jordan, the loss of land by Lebanon, and the West Bank coming under Israeli authority.

As diplomatically as possible, the French dissuaded the Jewish leader from such a grandiose endeavour. They argued that concentration in the short term should remain on the Egyptian problem. At first, Ben Gurion was annoyed by such insistence, but he reluctantly came to accept the matter at hand. However, when he realized that the initial move in the Challe plan would involve an Israeli attack on Egypt, he demurred — in part because he feared the "danger of Soviet volunteers coming to the Middle East."[84] He also "expressed his fear that if Israel launched the attack, the world would denounce her as the aggressor."[85]

For a time, the participants in the gathering appeared to be deadlocked over these objections — their differences too great to easily bridge. It fell to Israeli General Moshe Dayan to broach a compromise. He did so, tentatively, but ultimately with success.

Dayan knew that unless Israel acted first, Britain and France would lose their pretext for rushing to Egypt to "protect" the canal. He was also acutely sensitive about having his nation tabbed as the aggressor. And in the back of his mind was his innate mistrust of both France and Britain, the latter in particular. He was never really sure if either nation would hold to the plan long enough to launch attacks, and he did not want to be left high and dry if they backed out. To that end, he announced his intentions.

Dayan's proposal would involve "Israel opening hostilities with a kind of large-scale but limited operation and not a full-scale offensive; that way, if the British changed their minds at the last minute, Israel could retreat and walk away from the affair, claiming that it had done no more than embark on an extensive reprisal raid."[86]

Before the British came on side, Christian Pineau flew to London and, with Lloyd, went over the terms of the protocol with Eden. Then, with his prime minister's concurrence, Patrick Dean headed the British contingent back to Sevres. There, at long last, the events protocol was drawn up and signed by those representing the nations involved: Ben Gurion for Israel, Mollet for France, and Dean for Great Britain. Each of the three got his own copy, and then all returned home.

It was not until they had a chance to confer with Dean that Eden and Lloyd learned of the signing of the protocol. Eden had been adamantly against putting anything in writing, presumably because he knew that sooner or later, word of the collusion would leak out. He personally would not have put his signature to anything, but apparently he had not made this clear to Dean. (Lloyd likely would not have made such a mistake.) Dean had signed, certainly without realizing he was acting contrary to the specific but hitherto unspoken wishes of his prime minister.

In Britain, the Sevres alliance would soon be condemned, "mainly from the fact that the deception was aimed at the citizens of the United Kingdom."[87] Further, it would soon be "perceived as base and fundamentally negative in Britain, not because of the actual war plans, but because of Anthony Eden's attempt to hide its existence from the British public and from the entire world through half-truths and even outright lies."[88] Later that autumn, Eden went so far as to lie about the pre-arrangement in the House of Commons. Opposition Leader Hugh Gaitskell had questioned him about the matter, and the Prime Minister replied: "I want to say this on the question of foreknowledge, and to say it quite bluntly to the House, that there was not foreknowledge that Israel would attack Egypt — there was not."[89]

As soon as Eden learned that there were at least three copies of the signed protocol, he did his utmost to get rid of them. He took the one that Dean brought back and tore it into shreds. Then, in a rather high-handed way, he ordered the diplomat to fly back to France and get the other two copies. Dean did return to the continent, but came back empty-handed. The French were persistently non-committal as far as the whereabouts of their document was concerned, and Dean learned that Ben Gurion had folded up the one he had, put it in his pocket, and returned to Israel. Today, these originals are in archives in the countries involved.

In Britain, Anthony Eden was not the only official who was sensitive and secretive about Suez. Foreign Secretary Selwyn Lloyd was equally closed-mouthed, both at the time and two decades later in his memoirs. His account of the whole affair, written in 1978, can be seen as a valiant but ultimately flawed attempt at self-justification. He claims he did what had to be done, as did the Eden government, but he splits hairs to prove his point, particularly on the question of collusion.

Lloyd even goes on at some length about the dictionary meaning of the word. Then, when he finds his argument is still too weak, he brings in his views on Gamal Nasser, who "was an enemy" who governed by using "incitements to insurrection and murder."[90] In essence, he called Nasser a bad man, just as George W. Bush did of Saddam Hussein in an equally suspect attempt to justify another war a half-century later. Because Nasser was a bad man, it was, according to Lloyd, necessary to go to war against him.

But when he turned to the question of whether Britain colluded, Lloyd, like Eden, lied about it: "I do not myself believe that there was any binding agreement between the Israeli and the British governments."[91]

Surely David Ben Gurion, with the signed protocol in his pocket, would have begged to differ.

During this period, Lester Pearson, working and travelling between Ottawa, New York, and Europe, watched the clouds of war gathering over Britain and France. He was in London on September 3 and at the time talked privately with Selwyn Lloyd about the Suez problem. What

Lloyd said was, to a degree, a hint of what was to come, though Pearson could not have been aware of it at the time.

In a report on the discussion that he sent to Prime Minister St. Laurent, Pearson criticized the way Britain was handling its current difficulties. "The U.K. Government are not being very skilful in their management of ... international problems,"[92] he stated. Then, referring to the movements of British and French troops to Cyprus, Pearson pointed out that they "were not explained to public opinion," with the result that there was "a lack of imagination and skill on the part of those concerned ... with the public relations of U.K. policy moves."[93]

Pearson listened as the British Foreign Secretary went on about what Israel might do in the face of the nationalization and, by implication, about problems with Egypt in general. "Lloyd also wondered whether," Pearson told St. Laurent, "if things dragged on, Israel might not take advantage of the situation by some aggressive move against Egypt. He [Lloyd] seemed to think that this might help the U.K. out of some of her more immediate difficulties."[94]

The Canadian diplomat was shocked by Lloyd's suggestion that Britain would perhaps welcome an Israeli offensive against Nasser. A little later on, when the deed actually happened, Pearson was aghast, and the tone of his remarks in his autobiography bears that out. "It never occurred to me," he wrote, "that there was already a plan supported by the French for an Israeli attack on Egypt, and that the British would soon be involved."[95]

Within a short time, the Sevres Protocol had become part of history. By this time as well, the Anglo-French appeal to the UN Security Council about Suez had gone nowhere. As expected, the Russians vetoed the measure. They had agreed to build Nasser's dam, and now they were in no mood to ease the angst of Britain and France over what Nasser might have done since then. There were also other momentous events underway in the East Bloc empire, and the Soviets were dealing with matters that were much closer to home.

The Hungarian Revolution, as it became known, took place in the fall of 1956. It was an uprising against the totalitarian Soviet rule that existed in Hungary, developing after the ultimately futile attempts of a former premier to ease the oppression. Imre Nagy was a Hungarian

Communist leader who, after he became premier of the country in 1953, had become increasingly critical of the dictates from Moscow. Because of his views, he was removed from power in 1955, and the popular revolt against the Soviets gained credence shortly thereafter. Hoped-for reforms were brutally crushed, and many lives were lost. One of these was Nagy's. His Communist bosses had him put to death as a reprisal for his courage in trying to gain more autonomy for his homeland.

The bloodshed in Hungary, terrible as it was, did not get the attention of the Western world that it undoubtedly should have. The United States was in the midst of a presidential election. Britain and France were deeply involved in their own concerns over Suez, and most of the rest of the non-communist world was more attuned to the Egyptian situation. Events behind the Iron Curtain, significant as they were, simply did not have the same chord of awareness that they might have had, indeed, should have had. In the United States, Canada, Australia, and elsewhere, the possibility of a third world war over Suez was terrifying. The same fears were just not there when it came to what was happening in Hungary.

On the streets of Canada during the fall of 1956, there was much talk of war. As a university student at the time, I can well recall the endless discussions about Suez. We more or less expected that Canada would back Britain, because we always had; if Britain went to war, so would we. Many of us felt that some kind of military draft was probably inevitable. In conversations over coffee, whether one would heed the call was often a matter for heated discussion. Would there be a deferment — and if so, under what conditions? In the halls of academe, what would happen over the Suez Canal was exciting indeed. At the same time, it was an ongoing worry.

But senior high school, college, and university students were not the only ones worried. Our leaders in Ottawa were deeply concerned as well. As might be expected, one of those was Lester Pearson. He was working in every way he could to bring some kind of peaceful resolution to the Suez matter, and, at the same time, he had to decide what to do about Hungary. He did what he could, within the constraints that being from a middle power entailed. Nevertheless, the situation in Egypt, not Hungary, took most of his attention.

CHAPTER NINE

Fighter Jets and War

IN LATE SEPTEMBER 1956, Canada agreed to sell twenty-four F-86 fighter jets to Israel. The negotiations that led to the deal had been drawn out and complicated, particularly because the planes were going to a part of the world that was volatile at the best of times. Because of the Czech arms deal to Egypt, Israel felt particularly threatened, and while Canada was averse to taking sides in any dispute between the two countries, the existence of the Jewish state was precarious at the best of times. The matter was resolved when the Israelis indicated that the jets they were buying would be used for defensive purposes only. How Ottawa intended to enforce such a requirement was never explained.

The deal was known to Washington; indeed, because of the United States' position as the major power in the West, approval from the Americans had been sought and received. There had also been several earlier inquiries from South American countries for such planes, but the Cabinet at the time had been cautious about the intended recipients. Sales of this kind were dramatic, and the media found them easy to highlight. The planes were, for example, much more newsworthy than the truck parts that had been sold to Indochina the year before. Even a radio transmitter that South Korea purchased was ignored by the press because it was ostensibly for civilians alone. Fighter aircraft sales, on the other hand, were always of concern because of their end use, and also because such transactions could be politically risky.

Negotiations for the sale and the proposed delivery of the planes had become far more convoluted than had probably been expected at the outset. For one thing, Ottawa learned that the Americans were in the process of supplying Israel with military equipment at the same time, but they really did not want the public to know about it. On the morning of August 20, for example, Tyler Thompson, a minister at the American embassy in Ottawa, received a rather unusual, bluntly worded telegram from his superiors in Washington, which mentioned that the United States was in the process of supplying Israel with five helicopters, fifty half-tracks, and two hundred machine guns.

The telegram went on to say, "We need to be clear that there is full understanding between the United States and Canadian Governments that if our action becomes known publicly despite our efforts to keep it quiet, the Canadian Government will not cite our action as justification for any decision it may reach re sale of F-86's."[96] In other words, Canada could take any flak that might be forthcoming due to the aircraft sale, as long as no one in this country had the temerity to tell the press that the Americans were up to the same kind of thing.

Shortly after receiving the note, Thompson went to see Canadian Under-Secretary of State for External Affairs Jules Léger at his Ottawa office. Léger read the communication, and he in turn told Mike Pearson about it in a message stamped "Top Secret." Later on, the Cabinet did agree to do as the Americans wished, even though, as Pearson pointed out during discussions on the affair, staying quiet about it "was quite unrealistic because as soon as the [export] permits were approved, the sales would become public knowledge."[97]

Subsequently, after the sale to Israel was formalized and the Israeli government had paid for the first eight planes, another drawn-out series of negotiations began over the immediate availability of the machines. Then the number of aircraft that would be in the first shipment came into question. Finally, after much senior-level discussion, both here and in Israel, it was agreed that four planes per month would go to Israel. However, even after that major hurdle was overcome, there were yet more complications around the actual delivery of the jets.

At first, it was felt that Royal Canadian Air Force pilots would fly the F-86s at least part of the way. This was because, as Israeli ambassador Michael Comay pointed out to Pearson, "Israel did not have pilots sufficiently experienced in the operation of the F-86 to undertake trans-Atlantic flight."[98] Nevertheless, Israel wanted the planes as quickly as possible and hoped most of them would be delivered during the last months of 1956. Canada pointed out to the Israelis that the RCAF would not undertake ferry flights across the North Atlantic in the winter. It was just too dangerous to fly the single-engined F-86s such long distances over water in extremely unpredictable weather, with nowhere to put down in case of emergency.

Much discussion also ensued relative to the testing, dismantling, and then crating of the planes at the Canadair plant in Montreal, should a decision be made to send them by sea. Such delivery would obviously involve a great deal of time, and even after the crates were eventually delivered, the machines would have to be unpacked, put back together, test-flown, and certified before they would be operational. And there were other inherent concerns with regard to a crated delivery. As Pearson explained: "As soon as crates of F-86's leave the Canadair plant destined for Israel the fact may well become known to the public."[99] So much for the desired secrecy.

Canada also did not want news of the sale of planes to Israel to become public knowledge just when the Suez Canal problem was before the UN. Our selling of arms to one party in the dispute would reflect poorly on us as far as world opinion was concerned.

Still another problem arose. The Air Force was concerned over how, in case of a fatal crash when a plane was being delivered, they would explain to a rather bewildered public just why it was that a Canadian military pilot was flying a fighter jet belonging to the armed forces of another country. With this in mind, the senior RCAF officer in Ottawa at the time, Air Marshall C.R. Slemon, decided to flatly reject having his people deliver the aircraft at all. In doing so, he also took into account a necessary refuelling stop in Iceland of Israeli-owned planes with Israeli markings, flown by Canadians. He reasoned that the "problem of passage through Iceland ... would be difficult regardless of markings."[100] And if one of the planes happened to crash there, the resulting red tape would make any investigation of the matter absolutely horrendous. In other words, the RCAF was not about to drag yet another country into a quagmire that was already becoming an international headache. The Israelis protested that Slemon's refusal was politically motivated, but the decision was allowed to stand. In time, however, all of the machinations became irrelevant because of a surprising development that shook the world.

At 3:00 p.m. on Monday, October 29, 1956, Israel went to war against Egypt.

Within a matter of hours after he learned of the attack, Prime Minister Louis St. Laurent cancelled the aircraft order and informed Ambassador Comay that his country would get none of the planes. If his nation insisted on their money back for the aircraft they had already paid for, then that "would appear to be a question between the Government of Israel and Canadair."[101] St. Laurent's statement effectively ended his government's commitment to the whole sorry affair.

The days immediately following the Sevres meetings had been ominously quiet in North America. The American election, as always, dominated the media coverage. Dwight Eisenhower was running for his second term as president; after a heart attack a year earlier, he had recovered fully and was expected to return to the White House. Nevertheless, his every move, every press conference, and even every golf game was reported on at length. The only thing not reported was his score. To some insiders in Washington, what Ike shot on eighteen holes was as closely guarded as the secrets that mattered.

In this country, the press flurry stirred up by the two conferences at Lancaster House had pretty much died down as well. There had been speculation and a kind of futile hope that the Suez Canal matter could be handled amicably, if not with the stratagems of the first users' conference, then with those that came out of the second. This viewpoint had lingered for a time, but the Canadian media had earlier attempted to assess the situation in Egypt from an Egyptian point of view. Newsman William Stevenson, a correspondent with the CBC, had gone to Egypt in the middle of August and travelled extensively there. His reporting ended rather abruptly, however, on August 26. That evening, he and a couple of others were in a bar at the Metropolitan Hotel in Cairo. Shortly after they sat down and began to sip their drinks, a waiter walked over and told Stevenson that he was wanted in the hotel lobby.

The reporter went out and was met by a young Egyptian military intelligence captain. After he identified himself, the secret service officer told Stevenson to get out of Egypt and explained that his presence was no longer desirable there.

"He was very courteous," the newsman recalled, "but he gave me no explanation for the expulsion order."[102] A little earlier, two English reporters had also been kicked out of the country, but Stevenson was the first North American writer to be told to go. He took a plane from Cairo the same evening, and was probably relieved later that he had done so. The next day, two more media representatives with ties to Britain were jailed because the Egyptians said they were spies. In London, the Eden government termed the accusations without foundation.

There were other occasional references to Egypt and the Suez in the weeks immediately before and after the Sevres meetings. Many of them had to do with the reaction of Britain and France to the manoeuvrings of John Foster Dulles in response to what had happened, and was happening, in Egypt. British and French annoyance with the American Secretary of State was even reflected in criticism in this country. In early October, for example, the Toronto *Globe and Mail* editorialized on the matter, pointing out that Dulles had "made trouble for Britain and France in every quarter of the globe — without advancing peace, or the hope of peace." Then in a bitterly pointed and ominous reference, the editorial added: "This has been particularly the case in the Middle East, where Washington's wildly erratic course has made it impossible for Britain and France to chart a firm one; and where, in consequence, a major conflict could break out at any moment."[103]

In Britain in particular, there was a groundswell of criticism of the Americans and of Dulles. "U.S. Secretary of State Dulles has become the whipping boy for national feeling of frustration over the Suez Crisis and a focus for rising anti-U.S. feeling," claimed an American reporter based in Britain.[104] Then, in a passing reference to the British prime minister, the same writer pointed out that Anthony Eden had "done nothing to quiet criticism of Dulles."[105] No wonder the animosity between the two great nations would soon increase.

At the United Nations in New York, there was always hope that the Suez matter could be settled without war. Dag Hammarskjöld, the reserved, hard-working intellectual who was Secretary-General at the time, never stopped trying to find a solution agreeable to all sides. In a private conference in his own office on October 12, he brought Selwyn Lloyd, Christain Pineau, and Egyptian Foreign Minister Doctor Mahmoud Fawzi together in what ultimately became a futile last-ditch effort at resolution. At the time, the four men believed they had made a modicum of progress. However, their talks went nowhere. The Russian veto ended the hope that diplomacy would prevail.

On the same day the four senior diplomats were meeting, there were two other, essentially opposing developments concerning the Suez Canal. Both were, if not surprising, at least not expected when they were made public. The first matter had to do with ship insurance rates that came into play immediately following Nasser's nationalization. The major firms who provided coverage for the global traffic in the canal had long feared that, should the waterway be blocked with ships in transit, or should the vessels themselves be damaged or sunk, there would have to be major payouts. To cover themselves, the insurers boosted their rates, sometimes far beyond what they probably should have.

The shipping companies complained, of course, and as canal transit continued with little obvious change, the insurers, rather surprisingly, backed off. "The announcement that ship insurance charges for Suez were back to normal is taken … as evidence that military action over Suez is now ruled out."[106] Such was the short-sighted point of view at the UN at the time.

The opposite feeling prevailed in Washington, however. After extensive consultations with his senior advisers, with his Cabinet, and with some of the most influential industry captains, Eisenhower made a move that was pragmatic and, at the same time, inherently pessimistic. Because he obviously believed that the route to the East via Suez was less secure than it might have been, he ordered fifty large oil tankers be built as soon as possible. The move was announced on October 12, but planning and preparatory work had been in place much earlier. During the mid-1950s, the relatively tiny carriers that existed were just not economically adequate for the long and tortuous trek around the Cape of Good Hope.

In initiating the move, Eisenhower, and by extension his government, showed that in the long run he felt he could not trust Nasser. In the short run, Nasser might be making all the right conciliatory moves, but to Washington, neither the word nor the long-term commitment of the Egyptian President could be trusted. In fact, the American government's decision on the tankers was believed to be "proof the United States does not expect a settlement from Nasser with satisfactory guarantees, and is preparing alternatives for when he blocks the canal."[107] In other words, the Americans had pretty well convinced themselves that sooner or later, the canal would be closed. When that day came, they wanted to be prepared.

Three days later, on October 16, the *Globe and Mail* editorialized on what it believed was the state of affairs concerning the canal, three months after Nasser's daring proclamation on that balcony in Alexandria. The paper drew attention to the nationalization, the moves of John Foster Dulles, the blather at the UN, and the two failed conferences. Then the paper declared that the Suez situation remained relatively unchanged from what it had been several weeks earlier.

"Now, as then," the editorial noted, "Egypt holds the canal in defiance of her international agreements. Now, as then, Britain and France are unwilling to let Egypt have exclusive control of the waterway; and are prepared, in the last resort, to use sanctions against her. Now, as then, the United States policy on Suez is a matter of mystery; nobody knows what it is today, still less what it will be tomorrow."[108]

But even if the American policy was a mystery, the British government wanted it known that theirs was not. In order to spread the word in the colonies, speakers from Britain travelled overseas and explained to interested audiences the intentions of the Eden government. One of these ambassadors came to Canada and lectured in several cities. Toronto was one of them.

At the Royal Canadian Military Institute in that city, the Earl of Dundee painstakingly reviewed the profundity of the turmoil in the U.K. He explained that Britain did not want to go to war against Egypt, and that a diplomatic resolution to the situation there would be better than resorting to the force of arms. Ironically, a couple of days before Lord Dundee made this pronouncement, his own government had wrapped up talks at Sevres and had in fact decided to resort to war.

Lord Dundee, however, believed that the West, and in particular Britain, had to be ready to defend its interests in the Middle East. He felt that Western nations had hitherto been too soft in their approaches. He explained that because of our gentle treatment of other nations, we had hurt ourselves. Now was the time to "make a stand in the Middle East," because "if we abandoned the Middle East and its 200,000,000 people and its oil we would soon be lost."[109] Then the former member of the British Parliament reminded his audience that we in the West had sometimes forgotten what kind of men and women populate the Middle East. Doing so had done us harm, he added, because "we don't always understand that these are an illiterate and backward people."[110] One presumes the good Lord Dundee had yet to visit Alexandria, Giza, or Luxor.

But regardless of Lord Dundee's assertions that a diplomatic settlement would be preferable in the resolution of the crisis in Egypt, that was not to be. The whirlwind advance by Israeli troops across the Sinai sands ended such wishful thinking with a shattering abruptness.

With the full backing of David Ben Gurion, the Israelis, under the leadership of Major General Moshe Dayan, had carefully planned and executed the dramatic move. And it certainly did not come about by chance, a fact that was evident within hours of its unleashing.

Detailed planning for the endeavour began as soon as Dayan got home from Sevres. By the time his plane touched down on Israeli soil, the swashbuckling general had more or less worked out the finer elements of what he wanted his troops to do, but to some degree, the overall operation had been ready for months in advance. Israel had long realized it would probably be going to war against Egypt sooner rather than later, and there were always plans at the ready in case of any eventuality. What happened now was in the details.

Sevres had also given Israel exactly what it needed. As early as October 8, a full two weeks before the Sevres talks even began, Dayan had held an Orders Group meeting with his senior officers during which he explained the probable approach for an attack on Egypt. He told those who were there that day that their task was "to bring about as quickly as possible the collapse of the enemy forces and to achieve complete control of the Sinai Peninsula. We should try and capture what we can of the enemy's weapons and equipment, but we have no interest in killing a maximum number of his troops."[111] Now, on October 29, less than a week after the conclusion of Sevres, the protocol devised there only added to the legitimacy of what Israel intended to do. The code name for the campaign was to be Operation Kadesh, a reference with historical significance to the Jews during their biblical wanderings in search of the Promised Land.

By the time the attack on Egypt was reported in North American newspapers, many of Dayan's objectives had already been realized.

CHAPTER TEN

The Sinai Campaign

THE OPENING CAMPAIGN in what has been called the Sinai-Suez War was a masterpiece of Israeli daring, resourcefulness, and surprise. And no wonder. It came about with the approval of David Ben Gurion, the most respected leader the Jewish nation had ever known. The founding father and prime minister gave his personal blessing for the attack on Egypt and the intricacies of the action, just as he had sanctioned the massive troop buildup in the days prior to it. But with a kind of mystical chicanery, the assembled soldiers were said to be preparing for an expected war against neighbouring Jordan. The ruse fooled Gamal Nasser; it fooled Nikita Khrushchev's minions in Cairo; and it fooled the President of the United States in Washington, D.C.

Eisenhower had been inundated with signal traffic of a sombre sort during the final days of October 1956. He had read the reports from the Middle East with an ever-increasing sense of alarm until his concern became palpable and he realized he had to give some kind of response. Because he was so preoccupied with his own presidential campaign, his concentration was fragmented, but neither he nor the world needed a Jordanian-Israeli war at this time. The Suez Crisis was ongoing, Hungary was suffering, and the Soviets were threatening nuclear war if the United States interfered in Egypt. With each passing hour, the tension grew greater. Finally, twice within a few hours, Eisenhower contacted the American ambassador in Tel Aviv, instructing him to alert Ben Gurion of the apprehension at the White House and at the same time to ascertain from the Israeli leader just what was going on. "I must frankly express my concern at reports of heavy mobilization on your side," wrote Eisenhower in his first message. "I remain confident that only a peaceful and moderate approach will genuinely improve the situation and I renew the plea ... that there be no forcible initiative on the part of your government which would endanger the peace."[112]

This note, classified as "Secret," was brought to the Ben Gurion home shortly before 8:00 p.m. on October 28. A while later, a second message arrived. Both were written just hours before Israel went to war with Egypt, but in both notes, the American President was referring to Israeli moves against Jordan. At the time, an imminent attack on Egypt was not expected by Washington. Nevertheless, H-Hour for that reality was fast approaching.

There were three main Israeli objectives for the move into Egypt, but initially, as far as the rest of the world would be concerned, only one was paramount. Under the terms of the Sevres Protocol, the Israeli action had to look as if it would result in a threat to the Suez Canal. Once the chance of such a threat had been reported by the media of the world, the British and French would play their role by rushing to "protect" the waterway. In so doing, they would be carrying out the commitment established at Sevres. The three allies expected that Egypt would defend itself as best it could.

And it did, but not for long.

The combined air and ground attack across the central Sinai was Israel at its best. While troops led by Colonel Ariel Sharon slogged through endless miles of unforgiving sand, just above their heads flew sixteen Dakota transport planes carrying some four hundred members of the Israeli 202nd Paratroop Brigade. The airborne soldiers were being carried on ahead, where they would jump from fifteen hundred feet near a series of mountainous crags at what was known as Mitla Pass. This was a desolate area made up of multiple defiles, or gorges, roughly twenty miles from the Suez Canal. The paratroops were expected to secure the area until the ground troops and the equipment they brought came on scene. Under the forceful leadership of Sharon, that did not take long.

The trek overland was a tough one: vehicles bogged down in sand, seized up, heated up, and gave up. Men dug, pushed, pulled, and cursed, all the while dreading the lash of Sharon's tongue. Sharon was out to prove to the great Israeli general Moshe Dayan that the advance would not falter. Dayan had done the planning; Sharon and those he commanded would do the actual trek across some of the most unforgiving terrain on earth. The men coped with heat, blowing sand, thirst, and fear of what might lay ahead. They were convinced they could push the Egyptians back, but a bullet fired by a retreating enemy is just as lethal as one fired during an advance. Death in the desert was never embraced.

By nightfall on the first day of the attack the Israeli advance reached Kuntilla, a dozen or so miles into Egypt. Along the way, the Israelis encountered resistance, but at first, at least, the enemy was more of a nuisance than a threat. Often the defending Egyptians "followed their orders [by] retreating into darkness without resisting Israel's attack."[113]

Still, Sharon pushed his soldiers relentlessly, largely because he had intended to be in place for the link-up at Mitla Pass within twenty-four hours. Indeed, he had somewhat recklessly assured General Dayan that this would be so. Bringing it about, however, meant pressing on into the night, when even progress during daylight would have been fraught with danger. Along the way, the Egyptians defended as best they could, but lost personnel and equipment in doing so. They did, however, inflict losses on the Israelis, largely through air attacks using Russian-made MIG-15 jet fighters and Vampire aircraft.

In time, Sharon found himself bogged down in an area called the Heitan Defile. He wanted to press on right away but had been ordered to refrain from doing so by Dayan. However, the impetuous and bull-headed Sharon ignored his general's orders and stormed ahead. "His decision to advance … caused needless Israeli casualties"[114] and resulted in a tongue-lashing from the general. Later on, however, "Dayan publicly faulted Sharon primarily for tactics rather than disobedience."[115]

While the successful Israeli march towards the canal resulted in big-print headlines around the world, including in Canada, other units of Dayan's army had objectives elsewhere. For some time, Egypt had prevented Israeli ships from entering the Gulf of Aqaba, the long finger of salt water between southeastern Sinai and Saudi Arabia. The Egyptians' successful blocking of the Tiran Straits at the mouth of the gulf severely affected the Israeli port of Eilat. This state of affairs was an ongoing irritant for Israel, so Ben Gurion, through Dayan and his armies, intended to rout the Egyptian defenders from their fortifications at Sharm el-Sheikh and Ras Nasari, the main defensive positions for the closure of the Tiran Straits. As well, the Israelis hoped to "create confusion in the disposition of the Egyptian Army in the Sinai Peninsula and ... destroy fedayeen bases in the Gaza Strip and on the Sinai border." [116] Ultimately, Israel succeeded in all its objectives. The details of the various campaigns, however, are beyond the scope and intention of this volume. For our purposes, the reaction of the world to the supposed Israeli threat to the Suez is the principal matter. The contentiousness and seemingly endless acrimony relating to the Gaza Strip would be in the news for decades after the 1956 war had passed into history.

At the time the Israelis crossed into Egypt and began to move steadily westward, President Nasser was in Cairo. It was there that he received the first reports of aircraft dropping paratroops near Mitla Pass. At about the same time, at dusk on October 29, some of his observers spotted Israeli army trucks approaching Kuntilla. The two messages convinced the Egyptian leader that the reports of Israeli troops massing along the Jordanian border had been merely a cover for what was really happening. It was Egypt that was actually under attack.

Within minutes of getting the two disquieting reports, Nasser went to his army headquarters and for the next several hours remained there, assessing incoming radio reports and conferring with senior military personnel as to how best to thwart the advance of the enemy. As a corollary to the planning that was done that night, Nasser, ever mindful of the importance of the Suez Canal, "ordered that there be no interruption of commercial traffic," because he "feared that any stoppage of shipping would be seized upon by the British and French as grounds for intervention."[117]

The continuing operation of the Suez provided the setting for a rather strange concurrence of events. Nasser did not want the British in Egypt, but their ships and the ships of other nations continued to move up and down the waterway without disturbance, while two battalions of Egyptian soldiers crossed the canal and advanced to the east to confront the approaching Israelis. Nasser's troops were slow in getting into the Sinai, however, because they were faced with bridge bottlenecks in getting over the canal. There were only two bridges for them to use, and on one, troop movement took almost twelve hours. On the second, the crossing took more than eight, so in the interim, General Dayan's better trained, more mobile, and better equipped forces were well on their way to carrying out the objectives they had been given. To a degree, Nasser was beaten before he even entered the war. For that matter, there were Egyptian troops at Mitla Pass, but they were not expecting to have to defend their homeland in such a dreary place at this time. Most of them did not want to be there, and in short order, few of them would be.

Regardless of ongoing and sometimes valiant attempts to prevent the Israeli advance in several locations in the Sinai and Gaza Strip, Nasser's soldiers were gradually driven back by their relentless attackers. Despite reinforcements that were sent to the front, despite air power that was used effectively at times, despite the fact that they were defending their own land, the Egyptians found that they had to withdraw more and more often. Ultimately, "at a cost of less than 180 men killed and 4 captured, Israel routed half of the Egyptian Army."[118]

The retreat by the Egyptians was not an orderly affair. Many of the young soldiers Nasser sent into Sinai were unprepared to meet the tough, battle-hardened troops they had to face. Many of them became leaderless early on when their officers were killed, surrendered, or fled the field. Lots of them had to cope with a lack of water, an inefficient supply line, and cheap Soviet weapons that seized in the sand.

Of the approximately 45,000 Egyptians who were in the Sinai or Gaza during the fighting, 2,000 or more were killed and at least three times that many were taken prisoner. The Egyptian soldiers who retreated often did so alone or in small groups. They often ran away without boots because it was easier to travel in the sand in bare feet. Many perished from lack of water, others got lost and died of exposure, and many were simply never heard from again. Ultimately, "not one Egyptian unit that was actually engaged in battle made an organized withdrawal to the canal."[119]

Occasionally, Egyptian soldiers, realizing there was no hope, took it upon themselves to surrender. Sometimes their actions took on a kind of tragicomic aspect that was rather incongruous in the circumstances. In one such desert encounter, the Egyptian troops found themselves hemmed in by an enemy who was both in front of them and behind them. In the heat of one encounter, the Israelis captured an Egyptian Jeep and some small arms. Not far away, two rather dishevelled looking soldiers stood waiting to give themselves up. The Israelis assumed that one of the two was the Jeep driver. That, however, proved not to be the case.

In order to avoid more bloodshed, the prisoners were ordered into the captured Jeep, given a large white flag and a written surrender demand, and then told to drive back to their own lines and instruct their commander to give up. The plan sounded good, but when the prisoners did not even attempt to start the Jeep, the Israelis realized that neither man knew how to drive. Finally, in exasperation, one of them was given an impromptu driving lesson, the Jeep was started up for him, and a few seconds later, the two emissaries set out, their flag flying high.

They immediately got lost — but still continued forward, because even though the driver had learned to steer the vehicle, he did not know how to get it to stop. This ultimately proved to be their undoing. Somehow, they missed their own lines completely and, instead, drove right into a rather surprised squad of Israelis and got themselves captured all over again. This time, their tour complete, they remained in custody.

Yet despite such not uncommon occurrences, Gamal Nasser was pleased by the way the war had gone so far. In the first hours of battle, his worst fears had not come to pass. His troops were up against the Israelis, but the French and British, despite their bluster, had not attacked. Though he did not know it at the time, they soon would. But first, they had to enact another part of the plan concocted at Sevres. This involved issuing an ultimatum to the countries at war.

Twenty-seven hours after Dayan's troops swooped into the Sinai, the ambassadors of Britain and France presented notes of protest to the Egyptian and Israeli governments. Even though Eden in London and Pineau in Paris would deny collusion in the matter, the notes presented were virtually identical. There were two main requests made of both parties to the dispute. A third directive involved Egypt alone, but its contents were made known to the Israelis as well.

The first requirement demanded of the belligerents was that they immediately cease fighting. The second directive ordered the repositioning of the troops of both sides: both were supposed to stay away from the Suez Canal. Because of their success so far, Dayan's troops had overrun the Mitla Pass area and, had they intended to do so, would have been at the canal in no time. Now, however, in accordance with Sevres,

Lester Pearson holding the Nobel Peace Prize medal after it was presented to him in Oslo, Norway, on December 10, 1957. Maryon Pearson was present for the occasion.

Egyptian President Gamal Nasser nationalized the Suez Canal on July 26, 1956. That action led to the Suez Crisis and the Israeli and Anglo-French attacks on Egypt later that same year.

Anthony Eden was the prime minister of England when the Suez Canal was nationalized by Egypt. In the autumn of 1956, Eden made the decision to go to war against Egypt in the dispute over the canal.

Photo: John Melady

The Suez Canal Company offices on the waterfront in Port Said, Egypt. The building was commandeered on the night the canal was nationalized and then fought over during the Anglo-French attack on Egypt. It eventually fell to the British.

Photo: John Melady

The Suez Canal and the harbour of Port Said, Egypt. The white building with the tower in front is a police building that was fought over during the Suez Crisis.

Lester Pearson and Dag Hammarskjöld conferring in the United Nations General Assembly on November 12, 1956.

Political reporter Blair Fraser claimed that Canada's reputation was greatly enhanced because we did not go to war in Egypt.

Canadian soldiers stand in formation upon their arrival at Abu Suweir, Egypt, in December 1956.

The Jeep in which two Canadian peacekeepers, a prisoner, and a police dog were killed following a land mine explosion on the Armistice Demarcation Line between Israel and Egypt.

Canadian military technicians examine what is left of the Jeep after it was destroyed.

Jeeps were painted white and clearly marked with the United Nations identification during the time they were used on peacekeeping duties in Egypt during UNEF.

United Nations watchtower used by peacekeepers along the Israeli-Egyptian border.

Canadian peacekeeper William Lemaire poses with Egyptian children following a swim in the Mediterranean. Local children often approached troops and asked for money.

Canadian peacekeepers relax during off-duty hours during their tour of duty along the Gaza Strip.

Soldiers who served with UNEF tried to make their surroundings as pleasant as possible, even in the desert. This is the entrance to a canteen within the Canadian camp near Rafah. The picket gate reminded some men of home.

Lester Pearson mainstreeting during his time as prime minister. His reputation as Minister of External Affairs helped him gain the leadership of the Liberal party.

Lester Pearson.

The author (left) with Geoffrey Pearson as he recalled his reaction to the news that his father had won the Nobel Peace Prize.

«Nous devons agir non seulement
afin de mettre fin à la guerre
mais aussi pour rétablir la paix...
Mon gouvernement serait heureux de
recommander la participation canadienne
à une force internationale des Nations Unies.»

Lester B. Pearson
Le 2 novembre 1956

"We need action not only
to end the fighting but to make the peace...
My own government would be glad
to recommend Canadian participation
in such a United Nations force,
a truly international peace and police force."

Lester B. Pearson
November 2, 1956.

Photo: John Melady

The words of former Canadian prime minister Lester B. Pearson as inscribed on the Canadian Peacekeeping Monument in Ottawa.

Canadian Peacekeeping Monument in Ottawa.

they were ordered to check their advance and stay a minimum of ten miles east of the waterway. The Egyptians, on the other hand, were to remain west of the canal, even though that would have meant moving back over the bridges they had so recently spent hours crossing. The third demand — the most contentious of all as far as Egypt was concerned — was "to accept the temporary occupation of Port Said, Ismailia, and Suez by British and French forces in order to separate the belligerents and to guarantee freedom of transit through the canal to ships of all nations."[120] The two countries were informed that they had to reply to the demands as dictated within twelve hours. If they did not do so, then the two major powers would set about enforcing the directives.

Not surprisingly, Nasser rejected the terms out of hand. Had he not done so, he would have been relinquishing the sovereignty of his own country. His reaction was expected, of course, and that was precisely what the British and French wanted. The Israelis, on the other hand, accepted the terms — as they had agreed to do in accordance with the Sevres Protocol. They had already gained everything they wanted anyway.

From now on, the war of steel would be accompanied by an increasingly strident war of words — many of which would emanate from United Nations headquarters in New York City.

CHAPTER ELEVEN

Bombing in Cairo

THE NATIONALIZATION OF THE SUEZ CANAL had led to immediate and frenzied discussion at the United Nations in New York. As the news of Nasser's daring proclamation swept the delegate lounges, diplomats reacted in a variety of ways. A few were incensed, others were delighted, many were perplexed, and some were shocked.

The French and British were, of course, furious at the unmitigated gall of the "Cairo Colonel." The canal was not his to claim; it was *theirs*. They had built it. They ran it, and they would decide on its operation, its maintenance, and its future. No Egyptian dictator would be allowed to get away with what he had done.

Canadian and American representatives were surprised by the move, but their reaction was more tempered. Of course, neither country owned the waterway, and Canada, in particular, made relatively little use of it. We might have been sending ships to all corners of the world, but our reliance on Suez was limited. We were, however, an integral part of the Commonwealth, and our closest kin within that organization did not see things as we did. Australia and New Zealand were as angry as Britain, while India laboured from the outset for a kind of international acceptance of the Egyptian move. Indeed, the often-loathed Krishna Menon, chairman of the Indian Delegation to the General Assembly, tried to cast himself as a kind of global negotiator in the search for a diplomatic denouement. Because he desperately wanted to be the power figure who "solved" the Suez debacle, Menon attempted to get men like Selwyn Lloyd and Lester Pearson on his side. He intended to use them to further his own aims.

In early September, Norman Robertson, Canadian High Commissioner to the United Kingdom, informed Pearson in a telegram labelled "Secret" that Lloyd was very critical of the part played by Menon at the first London Conference, where he ended up "making a fool of himself."[121] Menon had somehow confused what he wanted to do and ended up supporting the Russian position on the Suez question. By the time he realized his mistake, it was too late to correct it. He left the conference, sulking.

A little over three weeks later, he attempted to use Pearson as a conduit to Dulles. Menon thought Pearson could help swing Dulles to the Indian position and suggested that Pearson use his influence to that end. Once again, Menon hoped to be the diplomat who resolved the Suez Crisis, but Pearson did not intend to be pushed around, even though he thought some of Menon's proposals were worthwhile. In a note to Robertson, Pearson explained his reservations about doing the Indian's bidding: "Krishna Menon's ideas seem to me to be pretty constructive but I am disinclined to associate myself, however discreetly, with his activities, even to the extent of approaching Mr. Dulles as he suggests."[122]

For the most part, the Arab world backed Nasser, as did Russia. The former support was not surprising; the latter was a self-serving attempt to gain increased leverage in the Middle East. To a degree, the Soviets succeeded, and their role in the Aswan Dam construction testifies to this. But their unpredictability soon became a major concern, in particular in Washington, because Moscow almost always opposed whatever the United States supported. The Russians deviated from this pattern, however, when it came to the initiatives relative to the canal.

The United States submitted resolutions that "condemned Israel's invasion and demanded her withdrawal from Sinai. The Soviet Union, Egypt's ally, supported these proposals."[123] However, when the votes were taken, the British and French vetoed the resolutions because they wanted to gain time and to secure a greater foothold within Egypt. They hoped to regain control of the canal and, if possible, topple Nasser at the same time. They did succeed in getting into Egypt, but their sojourn there would be brief.

Almost from the outset, Canada, in particular Lester Pearson, worked behind the scenes to diffuse the crisis the nationalization became. Pearson was influential at the United Nations, where he had been president of the General Assembly. In that role, he was known, liked, and trusted. He also had many contacts among diplomats worldwide. Indeed, had it not been for a Soviet veto, he would have been named the United Nations Secretary-General,[124] a post he undoubtedly would have filled with great competency. As it was, Dag Hammarskjöld, the man who did get the job, was successful in the role and in fact died doing it. He was killed in a plane crash in 1961 while on a UN mission in Africa. He was succeeded by U Thant of Burma.

Fortunately, Hammarskjöld and Pearson were friends, though not in their private lives as much as in their professional ones. They respected, trusted, and, where necessary, relied on each other. This was amply borne out over Suez when both men laboured together to bring about lasting peace in the world. The two spent countless hours working through solutions to the problem, sifting the shades of meaning, assessing the probable reactions from the parties in the dispute, and endeavouring to come up with lasting compromises.

In assisting Hammarskjöld, who had more of a global responsibility, Pearson talked to every diplomat he knew at the UN, and often to those the New York delegates reported to back home as well. John Foster Dulles, Dwight Eisenhower, Anthony Eden, Harold Menzies, Christian Pineau, Egyptian Foreign Minister Dr. Mahmoud Fawzi, and Prime Minister Pandit Nehru of India were all known to him, and in some instances were long-time friends. Dulles and Pearson were not close, but the influential American was a man Pearson could talk to, disagree with, and yet not alienate. The two sometimes needed each other, and during the Suez imbroglio they came to a workable understanding of what could and could not be achieved. In fact, Pearson could often bring forth a resolution and have it accepted, whereas the same initiative, coming from Dulles, might not have gained similar backing.

Pearson spent a lot of time in New York and equally extensive periods preparing for New York and debriefing after New York, as well as spending untold hours on planes going to and coming from the UN. The man never seemed to be at home, a fact pointed out by his daughter Patricia in an article she wrote for a magazine after he became prime minister. "My father's increasing involvement in External Affairs and international politics meant much travel," she admitted. "Our family ... lived a life of comings and goings, of partings and happy meetings, full of pride, often full of loneliness, but always full of warm, rich family closeness that no amount of separation could destroy."[125] Even though her father was absent so often during his career, his daughter's pride in him and all he accomplished shone through.

As soon as Nasser rejected the Anglo-French ultimatum that grew out of Sevres, Eden and Pineau embarked on the next step in their designs for Egypt. Royal Air Force reconnaissance bombers began making passes over Egypt to assess the situation, the terrain, and the targets prior to the commencement of the bomb runs that would follow. Initially, the reconnaissance was in daylight, but when Egyptian MIG fighters started to harass the interlopers, the RAF operated at night instead. Finally, once the objectives had been identified, British and French bombers operating from Cyprus and Malta left to attack airfields near Cairo.

They had to be diverted for a time during the first sortie. It was not until the attack planes had crossed the Mediterranean and were well on their way to their targets that Eden was informed of a serious and immediate concern. The matter had to do with civilians who were in the way. And these particular civilians were not Egyptian.

During the autumn of 1956, there were hundreds of Americans living in Cairo. Some owned businesses there. Many worked for Egyptian affiliates of international companies. Others represented the U.S. in its various government concerns. Some were tourists who, for various reasons, had ended up in Cairo for much longer than a night or two at the international hotels that dotted the metropolis. Now, many of these foreigners wanted out.

Major streets in Cairo were clogged as the exodus from the Egyptian capital increased. Men, women, and entire families drove themselves or jammed into taxis and scores of ramshackle city buses for the trip to the airport. Once there, they milled around, confused, frightened, but reasonably orderly as they waited to board almost any plane for anywhere. They just wanted to leave Egypt as quickly as possible. And while these people were in harm's way, Eden delayed his attacks — but not for long.

Bombs dropped in Cairo and other Egyptian towns, and, as in all wars, innocent civilians died. As expected, Paris and London insisted that they targeted military installations only; Radio Cairo claimed the attacks were on civilians. At least four cities were struck — Cairo, Alexandria, Ismailia, and Port Said — but the majority of the first deaths were in Cairo. The city had a population of more than 3 million at the time, and in the opening night of the war, there were three bombing raids there. "In each raid the city was blacked out," wrote one reporter who was on the scene. "Flares from the attacking planes lit up the big white and sand-coloured buildings of the metropolis brighter than if there had been a full moon. The boom of heavy anti-aircraft fire encircling the city accompanied the three Cairo alerts."[126] Another correspondent in the North African town said that Cairo was preparing for "the onrush of history with a curious air of calm and apprehension." He noted that "groups of Egyptians [were] listening to bulletins coming over taxicab radios. News about invading British airborne troops was greeted mostly with a shrug of the shoulders."[127]

There were some Canadians in Egypt when the air strikes began, and while their numbers were not great, many of those who could decided to go elsewhere. They were given direction, flight assistance, and consular advice from Ottawa in doing so. The Canadian government also issued a travel advisory, not only for Egypt but for Israel, Jordan, and Syria. According to our Department of External Affairs at the time, no Canadian other than those on official business would be permitted to go to any of the four countries in question. As far as is known now, the restrictions did not prove bothersome.

Other countries alerted their nationals as well, and a ripple effect of the Egyptian situation spread across the world. In the United States, the air force stepped up what they called their "intelligence watch." At the same time, the big air carrier Pan American announced that on an interim basis, it would not be flying into Damascus, Syria, but would continue as usual to both Turkey and Iran. The Madrid government announced that all Spanish ships were to avoid going anywhere near Egyptian waters, while in Lebanon, President Camille Chamoun invited Arab heads of state to an emergency meeting in Beirut in order to consider the current Middle East situation.

Here in Canada, those with family in Egypt were concerned about their safety. In the era before e-mail, CNN, and satellite telephone capabilities, reports out of Cairo often elicited the worst fears from relatives in Montreal, Winnipeg, and elsewhere. The Egyptian embassy in Ottawa was inundated with calls from worried expats who had not been able to contact relatives. In many cases, only the arrival of a letter a month later erased such fears. Some Egyptian Canadians contacted members of Parliament for news, but such requests were generally a waste of time. Few members of the House of Commons knew more than constituents in their ridings.

On Bay Street, the news from Egypt had immediate repercussions. Trading was brisk enough at the stock exchange, but the market suffered. This was particularly so in oil stocks and gold. On the other hand, copper, lead, and zinc all traded higher. In New York, Paris, and London, cottons and grains rose considerably as well. The reason for the volatility, one paper reported with rather obvious conviction, was that "traders reacted nervously to the Middle East crisis."[128]

The first bombings were not as militarily effective as the British and French planners had hoped. For one thing, the night attacks at the outset lacked a lot of the accuracy that was intended. But they were effective in another way, because they frightened the civilians who had to endure them. In fact, those who planned the attacks at the Cyprus-based headquarters "warned the Egyptians what the Anglo-French airmen were going to do before they did it, with the double purpose of preventing casualties and spreading despair."[129] How much despair was spread in the first attacks is still a matter of conjecture. Later sorties, however, were more feared. By that time, targets were hit with improved precision. This was particularly true of air bases where Egyptian fighter planes were located. The attacking forces had hoped to destroy as many as possible of Nasser's planes before they even had a chance to leave the ground. To this end, the Anglo-French assault succeeded.

The British and French, or the Allies, as they came to be called, were particularly concerned with Nasser's continued success in spreading propaganda about the attacks, about how unfair they were and how Egyptian morale was high in spite of the suffering his people were enduring. The main organ of this dissemination was Radio Cairo, and Nasser used its facilities to good effect. One of his biographers pointed out that "the average Arab waited for Nasser's speeches like a groupie. He became an icon and an incomparable speaker."[130] It was little wonder then that the President was able to command the attention of the populace in time of war, when his homeland was under attack.

At first, the Allied planners were reluctant to use their bombers to destroy Radio Cairo, as they erroneously believed its transmitters were in a heavily populated area. They held back because of the civilian losses this might cause; that would only help Nasser in his propaganda war. However, once the precise location of the transmission towers was determined, concentrated bombing followed. As it turned out, the towers were well out in the desert, in an area that was not populated at all.

As many as eighteen Canberra bombers "attacked the transmitters at high speed and low altitude during daytime. No ordnance hit the complex itself but one bomb struck an antenna, disabling Radio Cairo for several days before technicians succeeded in erecting another mast."[131] Shortly thereafter, Nasser was back on the air, more brazen than ever.

The first raid by RAF forces was actually led by a Canadian from Fredericton, New Brunswick. Wing Commander W.J. Burnett had served with the Royal Air Force for almost twenty years, and because of his rank and experience he had been selected to lead the squadron of Valiant bombers sent to Egypt. The focus for the attack was an airfield at El Maza, between Heliopolis and Cairo.

The planes made two runs over the target in order to assess the area and then came in on their bombing runs. The forty-year-old officer remarked that the outlines of Cairo were obvious from the air, but no street lights were visible at all. "Conditions were ideal for the attack and we recorded all the bombs within the target area," Burnett reported. "There was a certain amount of firing from light anti-aircraft guns, but it seemed erratic."[132] Then, their bomb bays empty, the attackers headed north towards the Mediterranean.

By this time, a full-out assault on Egyptian planes on the ground was underway. Waves of attacking aircraft arrived over Egypt, sought out their objectives, and, in relatively short order, rendered Nasser's air force incapable of retaliation. Some Egyptian fighters were flown out of danger to Luxor, in Upper Egypt, or in some cases even to Saudi Arabian airfields or bases in nearby Syria. Had they not escaped, they would have been destroyed by the attacking Allies. It was not long before "the Egyptian air force was grounded or took itself off. Of the planes which stayed, upwards of 200 [were] destroyed on the ground [and] the Egyptian air arm had been totally paralyzed."[133]

Now, world opinion would become a major factor in the further pursuit of the war. In that regard, what happened next was not Anthony Eden's finest hour.

CHAPTER TWELVE

The Canadian Reaction

TUESDAY, OCTOBER 30, 1956, was one of Louis St. Laurent's most depressing days in power. The affable, scholarly, mild-mannered "Uncle Louis" had been labouring quietly in his office in the East Block on Parliament Hill, signing the myriad items that came before him, conferring with his most trusted aides, and doing all he could to work through his government's concerns as they pertained to Canada and to the world at large. Suddenly, the relative calm of the afternoon was shattered when a staff member rushed in and handed him a news bulletin with a London dateline. The Prime Minister took it, read it, and reacted to it with surprise, disquiet, and what the Washington correspondent for the *Economist* would later call "uncharacteristic rage."[134]

The news item concerned the Anglo-French ultimatum that had been delivered to the Israelis and the Egyptians, telling them to pull back from the Suez Canal Zone or England and France would resort to war to see that they did. The matter had just been announced in the British House of Commons and had been picked up quickly by the major wire services.

Shortly afterwards, the first official word on what was afoot arrived in Ottawa in the form of a letter from Anthony Eden to St. Laurent. The message was stamped "Top Secret and Personal," and it was ten numbered paragraphs long, some of which consisted of single sentences. The overall tone of the note was self-serving, chilly, and highly presumptive with regard to the desired Canadian reaction. It also represented an obvious and immediate threat to peace in the Middle East, and perhaps to the world at large.

St. Laurent was aghast. He read and re-read the document, then grabbed the phone on his desk and called Lester Pearson, who happened to be in his own office on the same floor of the building. The Prime Minister shouted into the phone and asked his External Affairs Minister to come immediately. Pearson dropped the work he was doing, hustled down the hall, and within a couple of minutes was standing before a very angry St. Laurent. Pearson was taken by complete surprise when he noticed the obviously agitated appearance of the Prime Minister.

"I had never before seen him in such a state of controlled anger; I had never seen him in a state of any kind of anger," Pearson recalled. "He threw me the telegram and said: 'What do you think of this?' [The message] tried to justify the Anglo-French action and seek our sanction of it."[135]

Pearson took Eden's letter and, while St. Laurent paced the floor and fumed in the background, quickly skimmed through it; recognizing its obvious importance, he began to slowly and carefully consider it point by point. The more he read, the more annoyed he got. In no time, both men found themselves not just sharing similar reactions but expressing their mutual disbelief and shock at what the note was relaying and what Eden had done.

Both Canadians knew Anthony Eden, liked him, and respected him. They were also equally cognizant of his diplomatic background, his unsullied reputation, and his hitherto calm reactions in the face of international turmoil. The message in hand seemed to be completely out of character with the way the British statesman generally acted, and, of potentially greater import, with any decision he had ever made. And this decision, or at least the intent of it as conveyed in the note, impacted on not only Egypt and Israel, but on the world.

Once these two most important statesmen in the Government of Canada succeeded in calming themselves down a little, they began to reflect on the points Eden had made and then to consider what reaction they and their administration might have to them. Initially, St. Laurent was so incensed, he was ready to write a blunt, angry response, telling Anthony Eden to, in effect, go to hell; as Pearson put it later, a bit more diplomatically: "Mr. St. Laurent was prepared to send a pretty vigorous answer."[136]

But in any event, an immediate reply to the note was necessary.

Eden had opened his letter by telling St. Laurent, "As you know, for a long time the Middle East has been simmering. Now it is boiling over."[137] Then he went on to explain how his own government intended to stoke the fire under the boiling pot.

He reminded his Canadian counterpart that for some time, Israel had appeared to be close to launching an offence against Jordan, and that the United Kingdom, for treaty reasons, regarded such an endeavour with alarm. Now that they had attacked Egypt instead, Britain was under no treaty obligation to assist. Britain had stressed, however, that the belligerents must not end up blocking the Suez Canal, and that they must pull back from its banks. Should the waterway be threatened, Britain and France "would take any military action necessary to compel each party to conform." The two countries would do so, as Eden claimed, "because this war must be stopped before it has time to develop into a wider conflict involving others."[138] The note ended with Eden's patronizing comment, which said, in part: "I know we can look for your understanding and much hope for your support…"[139]

This last remark was as offensive to St. Laurent and Pearson as the information that preceded it. Eden simply assumed that Canada would unhesitatingly agree with and back whatever Britain intended to do. We had done so in the Boer War. We had done so in the two world wars. Now, in the light of those precedents, he simply expected us to do the same thing this time as well.

However, in commenting on what Eden had done, some historians believe there was another factor involved: "The British hoped that the Canadians would endorse their action but, fearing that they would not, had not bothered to inform them of its details."[140] And, as it turned out, the Americans had not been informed either. President Eisenhower referred to the matter in a television address to his nation. "The United States," he said, "was not consulted in any way about any phase of these actions. Nor were we informed on them in advance."[141] The American president was just as incensed about what had been done as his Canadian counterparts. And considering the fearful aspects of what Britain and France were doing, the United States had no intention of rushing to their aid. Instead, America began to work unceasingly to reach a peaceful and amicable solution to what could well have led to a global war.

But Canada and the United States were not alone in being ignored by Britain and France when they went to war in Egypt. All of the Commonwealth countries were taken by surprise by the move. In fact, "Commonwealth consultation, such as it was, had completely broken down."[142] This, in spite of the active support of New Zealand and Australia for Britain in its opposition to the canal nationalization the previous summer.

St. Laurent and Pearson knew they had to draft a response to Eden's letter. The two men gathered their senior advisers together, and the group reflected on what Eden was saying, then composed what Pearson called "a calm and courteous reply."[143] During its preparation, the document was revised several times. Each level of nuance was a measured one, and the necessary wordings were changed again and again. The group was particularly intent on ensuring that Eden would have little doubt of the Canadian reaction, that he would understand our displeasure, appreciate our caution, and know that we were not about to rush headlong into an abyss just because he wanted us to join him in doing so.

The Canadian reply was softened somewhat by St. Laurent's mentioning that he assumed Eden's actions were based on more complete information than was available in Ottawa. That may not really have been the case, but its assertion did temper the tone of the reply. The answer sent to Eden also implied that while Israel's move into Egypt might not necessarily have been justified, neither, perhaps, was the Anglo-French reaction to what Egypt had done or might do. In other words, posting forces in the Canal Zone was perhaps not the best way to settle the dispute and keep the belligerents apart.

The Canadian response included a warning to Eden about the possible escalation of the conflict should the nuclear-equipped Americans and Russians become involved. St. Laurent also mentioned that what Eden had done could well divide the Commonwealth, because all members of that body did not agree on the propriety of the action. As well, the Canadian response warned of a split between Britain and the Americans over what had been done. "This is a matter of deep and abiding interest to Canada," St. Laurent wrote, "the deplorable divergence of viewpoint between the United Kingdom and the United States."[144]

For good measure, the letter from Ottawa chastised Eden for ignoring the United Nations by acting as he had. "The fact that the action which you took was taken while the Security Council was seized of the matter is, I think, most regrettable."[145]

The letter sent, St. Laurent and Pearson felt they had done all they could at the moment. They had stressed the autonomy of Canada and had informed the British that whatever response came from Ottawa would be a Canadian one and would not automatically reflect the wishes of the U.K.

Of course, the entire situation placed Ottawa in an untenable dilemma. If we went ahead and supported Britain and France, wrote one historian, we "would risk antagonizing the United States, [but] if Canada opposed Britain and France it would be accused of disloyalty towards its two mother countries."[146] On the surface at least, there was no way for Canada to satisfy everyone. That would soon be obvious right here at home.

The *Globe and Mail* criticized the Canadian government for not taking a firm stand on the nationalization in the immediate aftermath of its happening. Now, with Eden's actions known across the world, the *Globe* supported Britain: "Britain intervened — and rightly so," declared the paper. "She has gone into Egypt not to make war, but to make peace."[147] In the same edition of the newspaper, however, an Ontario reader named E.S. Lavender took the opposite view and faulted the Anglo-French allies for their actions. The writer suggested that Canada should go to the United Nations and, on the floor of the General Assembly, condemn not only the actions of Israel but the stand taken by the French and British. If we did so, "such a stand would surely cause Britain, at least, to reflect on her folly,"[148] the correspondent added.

The Cabinet was also roundly criticized by reporters who wanted simplistic and clearly defined answers concerning who Canada was backing in the whole Suez matter. After one of several scrums with the media in the East Block, a visibly irritated Prime Minister St. Laurent turned on his heel and disappeared into the Cabinet Room. A minute or so later, he re-emerged and chastised several news people for their belligerence. "'It's too bad,' he said, 'that you can't come inside [the Cabinet Room] and tell us what to do. But we members of the Cabinet happen to be the ones who are responsible to the Canadian Parliament and the

Canadian people.'"[149] The chastising didn't do any good, of course, but probably St. Laurent felt better having said his piece. The hypercritical media people had little understanding or appreciation of what their prime minister was going through. And for the most part, they did not care. Not surprisingly, what they wrote and the way they slanted their reporting often elicited a negative reader response.

In a single issue of our national newspaper, several letters faulted Ottawa's Middle East stance and the fact that we seemed to echo the views of Washington. One writer, whose letter was published just before the American election, asserted that "in the event President Eisenhower fails to be re-elected … Messrs. St. Laurent and Pearson will have their foundations cut from under their feet. Serve them right."[150]

A Belleville, Ontario, reader dispatched a telegram to the paper that reflected on an earlier time when Britain and its colonies were one and their vast territories girdled the globe. "If Pearson's Whiggish views on Egypt are those of the Cabinet, and represent majority Canadian opinion," the writer pointed out with obvious disgust, "then the only decent thing for us to do is to get out of the Empire as gracefully as possible and be done with the pretence."[151]

Another reader, this one from Toronto, pointed out that there were "a lot of Canadians with courage, though you wouldn't think it from the utterances of those who run the pro-American Government in Ottawa."[152] Still another, who sided with Britain, wrote of matters that cause concern to this day. "It is time we got a party into power which intends to keep Canada free and maintain the great link of our British connections intact, no matter how it hurts Uncle Sam. He doesn't care how he hurts Canada, does he?" the reader asked. "Recent events, in trade policies and dealing with Ottawa prove this to the hilt. We need a revitalized party in Ottawa which can be Canadian in fact, and British-French too, a thing that would make even the great United States pause and consider."[153] Of course, whether the U.S. would "pause and consider" has always been debatable.

In the same edition of the newspaper, though, there was one correspondent who not only exhibited remarkable insight into the problem but suggested a possible solution to it: "In view of the fact that Britain is now, in the terms of the UN Charter, an aggressor, has alienated the opinion of almost the whole world, and has initiated hostilities which could develop into a major war, Canada should urge the UN to deliver a twelve-hour ultimatum to Israel, Britain and France, demanding the immediate evacuation of Egyptian territory. Failing compliance, the UN should brand these states as aggressors and immediately apply sanctions to any limit short of the employment of nuclear weapons."[154]

Several Canadian organizations that had strong links to Britain supported the mother country, as expected, generally with little or no reservations. These included the Toronto branch of the British Overseas League, the Sons of England, and the Sons of Scotland. The Grand Secretary of the then-influential Loyal Orange Lodge, Gordon Keyes, was unequivocal in his views: "We are still with Britain 100 per cent,"[155] he confided to a newspaper reporter.

In general, Canadian church leaders presented rational, tempered views on developments abroad. While most religious leaders were mildly sympathetic to Britain and France, they deplored the fact that the machinery of the United Nations was not more in evidence. The clerics who expressed their views publicly mentioned their personal fears of an escalating situation that could be worsened by the terrible weapons that were at hand. All hoped that neither Russia nor the United States would enter the fray because the use of atomic bombs was too fearful to contemplate.

Most church spokesmen — and they were all male — felt that the actions of Britain, while deplorable, must have been taken only as a last resort. All knew, or so they said, that Britain would have looked at all sides of the problem and would only have resorted to arms if no other avenue offered any hope of a lasting solution. Most Reverend W.F. Barfoot, then Primate of the Anglican Church of Canada, said it best: "Any resort to armed force, in any part of the world today, must be viewed with grave concern and is fraught with incalculable consequences. But it is to my mind unthinkable that those consequences have not been frankly faced by the British Government and the alternatives rejected because their consequences are even more dangerous to peace, justice and freedom." Then he added, "One thing we have learned not to expect from the Mother of Parliaments is irresponsible action in the face of known facts."[156] One wonders how Louis St. Laurent must have reacted to the clergyman's observations.

Then there were the public opinion polls, which, while not as sophisticated or as widespread as they are today, do give a glimpse of the views held by the Canadian public at the time. The snapshot of the nation was decidedly mixed. "A Gallop Poll showed that 43 per cent of Canadians thought that the Anglo-French invasion was a good idea, while only 40 per cent opposed it,"[157] observed the authors of one historical treatment of times. No wonder St. Laurent and Pearson were faced with such a crisis in their own country.

CHAPTER THIRTEEN

Paratroops at Port Said

ON THE MORNING OF NOVEMBER 5, 1956, the citizens of Port Said, Egypt, watched with alarm as waves of thundering military transport aircraft loomed low over their homes, and a vast array of parachutes suddenly blossomed in the cloudless sky. The early sun reflected off the planes, ancient Vickers Valetta and Hastings machines that had flown in from Nicosia, Cyprus. Fifteen minutes later a couple dozen French NordAtlases from Tymbou field, also in Cyprus, arrived. All had taken off from that Mediterranean island shortly before dawn. In all, over a thousand armed men jumped from these planes that morning and within a relatively short time secured the objectives selected for them. Because several ground-attack aircraft had preceded the drop and destroyed many of the rather rudimentary Egyptian defences, most of the men hanging under the canopies landed safely, gathered their chutes, and quickly got their bearings prior to fanning out towards their targets. The Anglo-French ground assault on the Canal Zone had begun. The British attackers descended to the airport; the French, to the local waterworks at the south side of the city.

The parachute drops were effectively constrained by the geography where they took place. There was not, and to a degree still is not, much to Port Said or to its sister city, the largely bedroom community of Port Fuad. Both are on the Mediterranean coast and are separated by the Suez Canal; Port Said is to the west of the waterway, Port Fuad, to the east. A long strip of land forms the seashore, and on it lie the sewage beds and disposal plant for the two towns, as well as a small airport the serves the area. In 1956, Gamil Airfield was only a few acres of flat land with two rather primitive landing strips and a small, makeshift control tower. The airfield is roughly three miles from Port Said. At the time of the air assault, what was essentially a shantytown lay between the airport and the city. Four cemeteries were to the west of these shacks, and a coast guard barracks was situated close by. This building was undoubtedly the most structurally sound in that area, and Egyptian troops defended it valiantly for a time.

Behind, or south of, the airfield and Port Said is a shallow body of water called Lake Manzala. Because of the lake, the boundaries of the town are quite restricted. Port Said has no remaining land available for expansion, nor, for that matter, did it have much at the time the Anglo-French forces landed there during the Suez Crisis. The town's raison d'être is the canal; in fact, without the waterway, Port Said likely would not exist at all. Aside from a few huts along the shore, almost nothing was there prior to the arrival of Ferdinand de Lesseps and his dream.

Even though there is train and bus service into the city from Cairo, Alexandria, and elsewhere, the best way to see the place is to arrive there by ship, as I did. The largely low-rise sand-coloured buildings downtown line the canal on either side and extend inland from it. On the Port Said side, close to the beach, is the base of what was once a large statue of de Lesseps. The statue itself, eerily similar to the one of Saddam Hussein that was pulled down in Baghdad, was smashed by Egyptians at the time of the crisis. The plinth that remains is both ugly and useless.

The canal mouth is between the two towns, and long cement breakwalls for it run out for about two miles into the sea. It is in this man-made basin that ships from all over the world come, jockey for position, and then slowly move in convoy formation into the canal itself. At intervals, other vessels emerge from it, having traversed the waterway from the south by way of Ismailia, Qantara, and Al Cap. The gathering of so many ocean freighters in one place is for some the only thing worth going to Port Said to see. I would disagree.

The tan five- and six-storey buildings that abut the harbour are reasonably picturesque and present to the world the same kind of shabby ambiance that was New Orleans before Katrina. I walked in the streets near the harbour, and my memories of doing so are of heat, noise, dust, and the clamouring of attractive youngsters asking for money. The pockmarked reminders of war are still noticeable in the walls of many structures. After all, this city saw fighting not only in 1956 but in 1967 and 1973 as well.

The main street of Port Said is Sharia Palestine, and it runs from the fishing harbour, near the remnants of the de Lesseps statue, along the west bank of the canal to the commercial basin, where ferry service operates between Port Said and Port Fuad. Just past the commercial basin is what is undoubtedly the most architecturally attractive building anywhere in the area. It is the Suez Canal House, the local operating centre for canal traffic. This was the building that Colonel Mahmoud Younes' men commandeered the night the canal was nationalized. The main police station in the city, a large sandstone edifice with an attached six-storey tower, is a couple hundred yards away, near the ferry dock. The police compound would ultimately be fought over by the attacking troops, but fortunately the building was not unduly harmed. Next to the Canal House, it is probably the most pleasant looking structure there today.

The canal itself is surprisingly wide as it passes between the port cities. And because the opposite sides are half a mile or so apart, there was plenty of room for Nasser to scuttle at least twenty largely obsolete craft (old freighters, tugs, and barges) in order to block the canal, thereby denying its use to the invaders. I was surprised during my research in Port Said to realize that the waterway was wide enough that the ship I was on had little difficulty manoeuvring in the inner harbour.

Today, downtown Port Said has all the facilities, services, and businesses one would expect in a town of roughly four hundred thousand souls. The usual port town customs offices, banks, travel agencies, and postal facilities are all there. A former Woolworth's department store on Sharia Memphis now sells junk jewellery, plastic pharaohs, and paperweight pyramids. The city does not attract a lot of travellers who want high-end products, but because it now has a rather malleable tax system, it has become a vacation place for Egyptians of modest means.

But the men in uniform who arrived there in early November 1956 were not there for the shopping. Nor were they there to find a place to die — and fortunately, relatively few of them did. Yet there were several close calls, a few injuries, and at least one fatality when a paratrooper came down on a land mine.

A couple of British soldiers drifted out to sea almost as soon as they jumped from their plane. Luckily, both were able to extricate themselves from their chutes and swim to safety. Another came down on the roof of the airport control tower, and though he was injured, he survived. A few landed on clusters of Egyptian soldiers who were shooting at them. There were injuries to the attackers and a handful of fatalities among the defenders.

The British airdrop at Gamil was expected to take about eight minutes (it took ten). The men parachuted at six hundred feet; their equipment (machine guns, radios, and the like) was dropped from a higher elevation. Luckily, no one was hurt by the equipment as it came down. None of the planes that brought the troops landed, nor did they attempt to do so, for three reasons: firstly, the airport was a battle zone at the time; secondly, neither runway at Gamil was long enough to accommodate large aircraft; and thirdly, the Egyptians had placed sand-filled oil drums along the Tarmac in order to discourage any pilot who might have chanced a landing.

The attacking force was aided by Seahawk fighter planes from aircraft carriers offshore. Several times the men on the ground radioed for air strikes, and these set the control tower on fire and assisted in the capture of the Coast Guard barracks. Unfortunately, the sewage system was also damaged and some raw effluent poured into the streets. This made fighting decidedly unappealing in places, so as soon as the defenders could be neutralized in such locations, the attackers repaired the damage. Nevertheless, the fight for Gamil was short, sporadically ferocious, and successful. In less than an hour, it was under British control.

Farther to the south, near the town waterworks, some five hundred men belonging to the French 2nd Colonial Parachute Regiment jumped into a confined area where scores of Egyptian troops lay in wait in slit trenches dug and reinforced for battle. The object of the drop there was to capture the water pumping and filtration plant, as well as two bridges that were the only exits out of Port Said to the south. French General Andre Beaufre wrote admiringly of what his troops did that day: "The dropping zone was only 300 yds. wide by 800 yds. long; to hit this confined space the drop had to be carried out from 300 ft. (the minimum permissible height) and the aircraft had to fly in two tight files at intervals of 50 yards with only 75 ft. between wingtips."[158] After some fierce and at times close-quarter exchanges, the French attained two of their three objectives. They gained control of the water system and one of the two important bridges. The other was blown up by the Egyptians in order to prevent its fall into French hands.

That same afternoon, five hundred more French soldiers parachuted into Port Fuad and in fairly short order took control of the city. They were assisted by air support from the same offshore vessels that had assisted the British up at Gamil. Ultimately, General Beaufre was able to write that at the end of the airborne action, "at the cost of some ten killed and thirty wounded … we had reached all our objectives in spite of enemy resistance, had captured some ten guns together with hundreds of smaller weapons and had inflicted losses of 500 killed, wounded and prisoner of the enemy."[159] The Anglo-French attackers had reason to celebrate. In his summary of the action, Beaufre neglected to mention that his men captured only one of the bridges.

IN THE DAYS JUST BEFORE and immediately following the Allied assault on Egypt, developments of a different kind were happening elsewhere in the world. In Ottawa, shocked by the belligerence of Anthony Eden's letter to Louis St. Laurent, government officials reacted as quickly as they could. As expected, the search for a satisfactory solution to the mounting crisis was led by the Prime Minister and the Secretary of External Affairs. Both men were still dismayed at the moves being made by Britain and France, and Pearson, in particular, would voice his consternation both at the time and long afterwards. In writing about the matter in his memoirs, he noted that for years he found it "impossible to discover any sensible explanation for the Anglo-French course of action."[160] Pearson went on to note that the air attacks on Egypt were effective, but that the gathering of great numbers of troops and the beachhead assaults that followed were not. In fact, he claimed that "the mounting of the Armada and the landings hardly seemed much of an improvement over Gallipoli [a First World War Allied debacle on the European side of the Dardanelles]."[161] He also touched on another aspect of the matter when he pointed out that the "ill-conceived and ill-judged enterprise also revealed a complete misappreciation of world response."[162] To a large degree, Eden never seems to have understood or even carefully considered how other nations might view or react to his actions.

Because of the breakdown in progress in the Security Council in New York, particularly in view of the draft resolution cited earlier concerning the American request for Israel to withdraw from Egypt, the whole Middle East matter was moved to the General Assembly for debate beginning November 1. Canada's reputation at the world body was a positive one, so there was little surprise anywhere that Canada would contribute in any way it could to forging a UN solution to the unexpected and ominous events occurring in Egypt. One afternoon when I was doing this research, I stood at the back of the General Assembly chamber and fell into a discussion about Canada's role at the UN over the years, and of Lester Pearson's role in the Suez debacle in particular. Shadrack Mbogho, a well-informed and helpful United Nations Public Information Assistant from Kenya, told me that in his opinion, "Lester Pearson's contributions here were as great as anyone else's, before or since."[163] This young man's world view, I decided at the time, was commendable. He laughed when I told him so.

In those first few days in November of 1956, while other nations also tried to decide how they would react to events in the Middle East, Pearson's first steps in dealing with the matter were taken in Ottawa, not New York. There were several ongoing consultations with Cabinet members and with External Affairs officials. Initially, there was a great deal of unease because the situation was unprecedented, and no one was sure how it should best be handled. Complicating the matter was Canada's support for Israel — or at least support for its existence as a nation — along with its real misgivings about Israel's decision to go to war against Egypt.

While some Cabinet members might have been inclined to agree with what Britain and France had done, particularly in the face of the provocation from Nasser, like St. Laurent and Pearson they were dismayed at the breach in important alliances. Most felt, however, that the Anglo-French adventure was certain to collapse without support from Washington.

Complicating matters further were the views of others beyond Canada. High Commissioner Norman Robertson cabled Pearson on November 1 and reported on a meeting he'd had with Lord Home, the

Secretary of State for Commonwealth Relations in the United Kingdom. Home was well aware of Canada's consternation over the Suez matter but still insisted his government be kept informed of Canadian feelings on the matter. Robertson stated that he had told Home that "the foundations of the relationship between Commonwealth countries had been severely shaken. The U.K. and France had somehow got themselves into a truly tragic position. Neither of them had any closer friend and ally than Canada, but at this pass I could not see what we could do to help."[164]

A little earlier, Dulles had phoned Pearson to complain because "for some days" Washington "had been cut off from all sources of information in London on British policy."[165] The phone call certainly got Pearson's attention, and he seems to have been particularly worried because Dulles was "in a state of emotion and depression"[166] at the time it was made. This was just before a personal crisis befell the hard-driving American Secretary of State. Early in the morning of November 3, he wakened with stomach pain so severe he thought he had better call an ambulance. He was rushed to Walter Reed Hospital in Washington, and "the diagnosis was soon made. Foster Dulles had abdominal cancer."[167] Suddenly, one of the great pivotal politicians of history might not be able to carry on. Even though Dulles laboured diligently for some time afterwards, the disease within him gradually took its toll. He died three years later, but by that time, the Suez Crisis was part of history.

During the worldwide drama the situation became in early November, Pearson took his direction from and offered advice to the Cabinet in Ottawa. This body met during the morning of November 1, at which time they gave their formal approval of the note St. Laurent had sent to Eden. They also listened as Pearson alerted them to the developments at the United Nations. Later the same day, the seventy-six-nation General Assembly was scheduled to begin debate on events in the Middle East, and Pearson told the Cabinet that he felt he should be there to ensure that the Canadian view was considered. In his stead, R.A. MacKay, Canada's permanent representative at the UN, could have acted, but after due consideration, Pearson was urged to attend himself. Once in New York, he would "seek the advice and assistance of his colleagues on the stand he should take."[168]

In the Cabinet extracts of November 1 a possible solution to the Middle East situation was hinted at. Several of those around the table knew that there was not unanimity in the U.K. for what Britain and France were doing and that "the U.K. government would soon welcome a proposal calling for the cessation of hostilities."[169] For the first time came the suggestion of "the provision of substantial police forces stationed on the Israeli-Arab borders to keep peace."[170]

Here was the solution that Pearson wanted and that he would pursue diligently in the hectic days that followed. Shortly after the Cabinet meeting ended, he ate lunch on the run and then was whisked to Uplands for the flight to New York. The next few hours there would be some of the most critical in the history of the United Nations.

CHAPTER FOURTEEN

Pearson's Promise

ANYONE WHO HAS EVER FLOWN into LaGuardia Airport in New York knows of the landings over the East River. As your plane comes in, you glance from the window and all you can see is water. Then, in a matter of seconds, you are on the runway. Because of its location, it is not surprising that fog at LaGuardia can be of particular consequence to the safe operation of the airport. That problem was a factor when Lester Pearson's Department of Transport plane from Ottawa arrived over New York on the afternoon of November 1, 1956. Later he explained that because of the fog his landing was delayed and he barely got to the United Nations in time for the commencement of the Suez debates in the General Assembly. Among the handful of individuals with him on the flight that day were Assistant Secretary of State John W. Holmes and A.S. McGill, the minister's executive assistant. Fortunately, the driver who took them downtown apparently set something of a speed record into Manhattan, and they arrived at the UN compound with just minutes to spare. Pearson and his colleagues jumped from the car and rushed inside just as delegates from all over the world streamed to their desks.

That day virtually every seat was full, which was indicative of the importance of the gathering but also of the widespread fear of what could happen if events in the Middle East were not curtailed, or at least managed in such a way that they did not lead to a global conflagration that no nation would win. As delegates settled in, there were conversations in a dozen tongues about the events half a world away. The apprehension of what could happen surpassed the shock at what had happened. In fact, the unspeakable threat of an atomic war was in the back of every delegate's mind. The terrible devastation of Hiroshima and Nagasaki was still relatively recent, and the plight of those cities remained as stark reminders of the horror that modern war had become. One nuclear bomb dropped on Cairo, London, Moscow, or Paris would be an unspeakable tragedy, not just for the city in question but for all humanity. No wonder Lester Pearson entered the General Assembly hall that day with an acute consciousness of the need to try to curtail the madness of men.

In recalling his apprehension at the time, Pearson admitted that the crisis could easily have engulfed far more than just the Middle East. If Russia had carried out its threat to use nuclear weapons should the U.S. become involved in Egypt, the aftermath could well have been devastating. Pearson and the other Canadians there that day knew this, of course, as did everyone else in the vast chamber. Ultimately, no one was immune from nuclear war — no matter where the weapons might have been used.

While they were together in Ottawa, Pearson and St. Laurent had discussed what they felt should be the Canadian position at the United Nations. Neither man had worked out in his own mind exactly what approach might be the most effective, yet instinctively, both knew that the ramifications of a wider war in the Middle East were too terrible to contemplate. Such an eventuality could well become real if the difference of opinion among world bodies worsened. As Pearson described the situation later, the crisis already "threatened to destroy Anglo-American co-operation, to split the Commonwealth, and brand our two mother countries, Britain and France, as aggressors."[171] A solution was imperative.

The possibility of some kind of an international police force to control rogue nations had been mentioned in several quarters in the years after the United Nations was formed. However, the formalization of such a body had never materialized. Now, Pearson felt, the idea should be considered again. Because he wanted to know where the British might stand on the matter, as well as how they would react if he made such a suggestion at the UN, he'd phoned Canada's High Commissioner in London that morning before leaving for New York. Norman Robertson would find out what the British thought of the idea so that if such a proposal were made by Canada, it would be given as much weight as possible.

Robertson acted immediately and within a short time learned that Britain liked Pearson's idea; he even found out that Eden would mention and lend support to such a proposal in an address to Parliament the same day. Robertson returned Pearson's call within minutes of getting an advanced transcript of Eden's speech. Pearson listened and then, with a feeling of satisfaction and relief, left for New York.

Four years later, Eden dealt with the item in his memoirs. Referring to the raucous Suez sitting in the U.K. Parliament that day, Eden recalled that he was asked for his thoughts on what was happening in Egypt. "In my reply to the debate," Eden explained, "I made the suggestion that a United Nations force should eventually be associated with the Anglo-French police action. This idea was taken up in the General Assembly the next day by Lester Pearson and others."[172]

Eden's words were the keys Pearson felt he needed for his UN submission. Eden referred to the fighting between Israel and Egypt and intimated that Britain and France could be the countries to place their ground forces in the theatre and keep the belligerents apart. However, he subsequently added a partial disclaimer that could be interpreted as a fallback if Anglo-French troops were not selected as peacekeepers. "If the United Nations were ... willing to take over the physical task of maintaining peace in that area," Eden told the House, "no one would be better pleased than me."[173]

And no one was more pleased by these words than Pearson and his Canadian colleagues in New York. In response, they set about drafting a possible initiative for presentation in the Assembly chamber. They worked feverishly, writing, revising, redrafting, and writing again as speaker after speaker went to the podium and outlined their own countries' concerns regarding the Middle East. While delegates from across the world voiced fears and alluded to potential solutions, all seemed to overlook one step the Canadians felt was vital. This omission ultimately led, not to the Canadian backing of the U.S. proposal, but to a decision to abstain from voting on it at all.

The American plan was pushed through, largely as a result of the bullying tactics of Dulles. He and his team worked the back rooms, buttonholed as many delegates as they could, and exhorted each to support the American idea. This manoeuvring went on well into the early morning of November 2. Dulles was adamant that his plan be adopted no matter what, as Pearson realized after a discussion with the American. "He told me of their resolution, that they were going to push it through and try to get a vote that night. He had become a statesman in a hurry," Pearson recalled. "I was disturbed by this, but it was apparent that there was no way to deter him and I did not try."[174]

However, when he talked to Dulles, Pearson felt that he should at least attempt to voice a couple of suggestions. He mentioned adding an amendment to the resolution that might place Britain and France in a better light, so that they would look less like the aggressors some countries were claiming them to be. Pearson spoke of the police force idea to Dulles and suggested, failing its inclusion, at the very least holding an international conference to assess the situation. Either might have helped restore the image of Britain and France in world opinion. However, Dulles turned a deaf ear to both ideas, and by this time "it was too late and too risky ... to try to amend the resolution that night."[175] The vote went ahead as Dulles intended. The American idea was adopted by a vote of sixty-four to five, with six abstentions, one of which was Canada's. Ultimately, the resolution went nowhere.

But the aggressiveness of the American Secretary of State was not the main reason Canada abstained when the vote was called. We also abstained because the Dulles proposal still lacked teeth. It called for a ceasefire but little else. There was nothing to prevent the belligerents from taking a respite for a few days, or even months, then, as soon as their arms and determination had been adequately replenished, renewing hostilities. Pearson and his Canadian team (Bert MacKay, Geoff Murray, and John Holmes) knew this and continued their efforts to obtain some kind of policing component that would step between the combatants, keep them apart for however long it took, and ensure that there was peace in Egypt.

As mentioned earlier, many media in Canada were displeased with what they regarded as the lack of a firm resolution over Suez by the Canadian government. They had been critical of St. Laurent over the matter and had angered him when they'd said so. And when Pearson flew to New York, they complained as well. Now, though, the *Globe and Mail* stumbled onto a possible reason why the Cabinet was proceeding cautiously. "Into the vacuum created by the Government's reluctance to decide on a policy came a flood of speculation after Mr. Pearson left the capital," wrote one reporter, who added, "If finally forced into a corner, the Cabinet might instruct the External Affairs Minister to abstain from voting in the assembly. The Cabinet … didn't make a decision because it didn't want to choose between Britain on the one side and the United States on the other."[176]

This reasoning was correct, as Pearson would later affirm. "We could not support the United States' resolution," he wrote, "and expect to get a sympathetic hearing in Britain. If we opposed it, our standing with other members of the Commonwealth, with the Moslem world, and with the United States would simply disappear."[177]

In other words, Canada was in a no-win situation. For that reason, Pearson, their former president, asked for and received permission to address the delegates of the General Assembly. He wanted to explain the reasoning behind his country's abstention.

He began his remarks with what he later admitted were several rather meaningless generalities. He said, for instance, that Canada had not enough time to carefully consider the American motion; that because of its importance, it should not have been rushed. Then, once these platitudes were out of the way, Pearson told the Assembly what his real thoughts were: that he believed that any potential solution to the problem in Egypt must contain some kind of policing proviso. He suggested that the Secretary-General should be given the task of pursuing such a possibility with member governments. Finally, Lester Pearson made one of the most important proposals he would ever make at the United Nations. He told the representatives of the world who were gathered before him what his country would do: "My own government would be glad to recommend Canadian participation in such a United Nations Force, a truly international peace and police force."[178]

Today, these words are inscribed in stone on the face of the beautiful peacekeeping monument in downtown Ottawa, a stone's throw from the Parliament Buildings. In all likelihood, the man who voiced them that day in the United Nations General Assembly could never have imagined the long-term, international importance of what he had just suggested. That short statement not only had a profound relevance to

Lester Pearson's Canada, it has had an irreversible impact on this nation and on the world ever since. Indeed, in the decades that have passed since Pearson's day, Canada has truly become a peacekeeping nation.

Pearson concluded his remarks, then stepped down from the podium and into history. Almost immediately, he was pleasantly surprised at the impact his words had had. The fact that it was almost 4:30 in the morning suddenly seemed irrelevant. It was as if the vast majority of delegates in the hall had been searching for a solution that would work for a problem that would not go away, a conundrum that had baffled them all. Delegate after delegate came over to Pearson's desk, congratulated him, and indicated their appreciation for what they had just heard. Virtually all of them would have to confer with their superiors at home, of course, in order to ascertain how they should vote on Pearson's plan. Nevertheless, the potential for a real solution to Suez had been voiced, and they intended to support it as soon as they had the acquiescence from their governments to do so.

Even the irascible John Foster Dulles was impressed.

Although he had more or less expected that Canada would support his proposal and was somewhat taken aback when he learned we would not, he was nonetheless clever enough and statesman enough to listen with care to what Pearson had said. The two men respected each other, and Dulles may even have admired Pearson for not being browbeaten into acquiescing to American demands. In any event, Dulles had listened, quickly evaluated the Canadian idea, and then leant his weight and prestige to it.

"When Dulles got up to move adjournment," Pearson wrote later, "he said that he welcomed this statement, and he asked the Canadian representative to formulate and introduce a concrete proposal for an international force."[179] When he heard these words, Pearson was elated.

By this time, every delegate in the room was dead on his feet, the Canadians among them. As soon as he could extricate himself from the congratulatory crush, Pearson went directly to the nearby Drake Hotel for a scant few hours' rest before the real work on his proposal began. And even though he was staying in what he sometimes called his favourite accommodation in New York, his sleep that night was both restless and brief. With the dawn came new challenges.

During the morning, as traffic roared up and down on Park Avenue and the cacophony of horns and hubbub that is New York went on as relentlessly as ever, Pearson and his colleagues tuned out the racket and concentrated on the task at hand. They began by assessing the situation in Egypt as it currently stood, then went on to envision what they hoped it could become if peacekeeping units of some kind could be placed there. The overall idea was a good one, and now they knew it could, and likely would, be adopted. But between the idea and the reality of it being implemented lay a thousand details, all of them vital, none easy to achieve. Then there came an obstacle where none was expected.

At noon that day, Pearson, Holmes, and MacKay went to lunch with Secretary-General Dag Hammarskjöld, the quiet pillar of strength who exemplified the best of the United Nations at the time. The austere, highly intelligent Secretary-General's first reaction to Pearson's plan was skepticism: he did not think it would work. The members of the Canadian contingent were not about to give up, however. They reasoned with Hammarskjöld as much as possible in a short time, finished eating, and left. Later on, when Hammarskjöld had had more time to evaluate the proposal, discuss it with others, and think it through, he realized its merits and became one of its most dedicated supporters.

But in the meantime, Pearson had rushed back to LaGuardia, caught a flight to Ottawa, and prepared to defend his plan in the Canadian Cabinet. If that body approved of the measure, he would then get ready to present it in the General Assembly so that the United Nations could collectively take a small step towards peace.

CHAPTER FIFTEEN

Protest and Problems

WHILE THE IMPORTANT and ultimately successful deliberations were in progress at the United Nations in New York, a series of diverse but interconnected events were taking place in other areas of the world. In London, England, the Suez situation was uppermost in everyone's minds, and the war effort of the nation was on the front page of every major newspaper in town. And because the war and all the entanglement involved with it were in the news, so were the actions of Anthony Eden and the things that he had set in motion. In the summer, the war had been only words. But now that England and France were dropping bombs on another country and the Anglo-French Allies had become international pariahs, people of every stripe took notice, approving or disapproving, rarely failing to express their opinion about what was happening.

In Parliament, in the streets, in the media, and in the pubs and clubs of the nation, the Suez war was as controversial as anything had been for years. There was a huge rally in London's Trafalgar Square, where thousands stood in a cold November rain and listened as speaker after speaker denounced Eden, protested for peace, deplored war, pushed and shoved, shouted and cursed, and demanded the nation alter its course. For every protest — and there were many all over the country — there was a counter-protest. In short, the people were as divided as Eden's initiative was controversial.

During what was perhaps the largest demonstration, the one in Trafalgar Square, Anthony Eden's wife, Clarissa, rather foolishly decided to see for herself what was going on. Wearing a head scarf and doing her best to remain incognito, she ducked out of 10 Downing Street and walked down Whitehall to Trafalgar Square to get a personal sense of what was happening.

Labour politician Aneurin Bevan was standing on a makeshift platform near Nelson's column, the focal point in the square. Before he rose to speak, the crowd, while restive, was not particularly boisterous or unruly. However the fiery Bevan soon had them stirred up, and in no time they were bellowing anti-Eden slogans, roaring approval of everything said, and agreeing with the speaker that the Prime Minister had to go. In his high, squeaky, shrill voice, Bevan reminded the crowd that Eden had declared that war was the price the nation might have to pay to settle the Egyptian question. Then, with a flourish of screaming rhetoric, the politician on the stand told the crowd what he thought of the man at 10 Downing: "If Eden is sincere in what he is saying — and he may be — then he is too stupid to be Prime Minister." The crowd roared. Bevan went on, "He is either a knave or a fool: in both capacities, we don't want him!"[180] The great crowd rose as one, cheered madly as Bevan stepped down, and stridently denounced the man who had just been vilified.

Then someone recognized the Prime Minister's wife standing alone. A few onlookers actually went over to her and, at first at least, seemed sympathetic. But "as this group grew in number, it was noticed by some of the main body of the crowd, who began to investigate what was going on."[181] As Anthony Eden later described his wife's little adventure, "She thought it prudent to return to Downing Street."[182] And well she did.

The vast square began to empty as the swirling mass of humanity sought an outlet for their pent-up frustration. By this time they had become, not an orderly British audience applauding a performance, but an unruly mob in search of a scapegoat. The ragtag human wave poured down Whitehall towards the Prime Minister's residence, where a meeting of Eden's Cabinet was in session. They barged ahead, screamed at the top of their lungs, and demanded satisfaction from their government. Fortunately, Clarissa Eden had walked away quickly and, shaken and wiser, reached her little street and the protective security of Number 10 before the crazed marchers could get there. At this point, she was barely ahead of them. Inside, where he was attending Cabinet, Selwyn

Lloyd noticed the racket outside; he later recalled "the noise of the demonstration … and then every few minutes a crescendo and an outburst of howling or booing."[183] Concentrating on the agenda for the nation became difficult, but Eden and his ministers ploughed ahead and tried to block out the racket from the street.

Outside, the angry mob moved purposefully forward, not caring to be civil. Many threw firecrackers at police officers and the horses they rode. Luckily, no one was trampled and none of the mounts panicked. "A young man tried to drag a policeman off his horse," wrote a reporter who was there. "Another leaped from a balustrade … onto the back of a policeman. Another struck a policeman."[184]

Luckily, Downing Street, which is not accessible to the public today but was when the Suez protesters approached, has a rather narrow entrance. Several of the mounted police officers formed up there and, despite enduring everything from firecrackers to spittle to personal assault, prevented the mob from reaching Number 10. The unruly protestors were wedged past and forced to carry their rage away. At the end of the day, at least eight mounted policemen were hurt, several protestors were arrested, and two of their ringleaders were jailed without bail. Fortunately, the integrity of the Prime Minister's residence was intact and his safety assured. There are no indications that Clarissa Eden ventured out again that day.

While the protests and the problems over Suez played themselves out in Britain, and to a much lesser extent in France, troops from both nations moved ahead with invasion plans for the Canal Zone. The long-delayed buildup of forces continued in Malta and Cyprus, as waves of planes involved in the bombings in Egypt flew across the Mediterranean skies. Elsewhere, some of the toughest troops in the world were proving to be unstoppable as they advanced into the Gaza Strip. The Israelis, under the inspired leadership of Moshe Dayan, captured Gaza City on November 2, and with it, the entire northern half of the Gaza Strip. At roughly the same time, contingents of his men slogged south along the Gulf of Suez to the desert town of Tor, captured it, and prepared to go on to Sharm el-Sheikh. The following day, all of Gaza fell to the Israelis. In both theatres, Dayan's soldiers fought ferociously, with a determination and a ruthlessness that was occasionally as controversial as it was effective.

Clearing harbour at Malta on November 3 were two of the larger British troopships, *Ocean* and *Theseus*. On board were Royal Marines, who would be central to the subsequent landings at Port Said itself. Another British ship of note was the Royal Navy's *Tyne*. It was the head-quarters vessel for the entire on-scene Suez operation and carried Task Force Commander General Stockwell and his deputy, French General Andre Beaufre. Their duties in the hours prior to invasion were oner-ous, complicated, and nerve-wracking, yet both men worked non-stop, co-operated reasonably well, and functioned with little sleep. They were undoubtedly well-chosen for the responsibilities given them.

The buildup of vessels for the Suez armada became more formida-ble with each passing hour. One ship in the fleet was the *Jean Bart*, a 35,000-ton battleship equipped with eight 15-inch guns. There were three large cruisers, one of which was a New Zealand ship, the *Royalist*. It, however, was subsequently replaced by HMS *Ceylon*, largely for polit-ical reasons (this war was not a New Zealand war). There were also a dozen destroyers, five of which were French. These included both destroyer-escorts and anti-submarine vessels. On board all were dedi-cated, keen, and superbly confident officers and men. This endeavour, they expected, would be short, sharp, and successful. They all believed that Egyptian resistance would not be a problem.

But there were problems on the other side, of a different kind.

During the campaign against Israel, the Egyptian resistance became weaker and weaker as Nasser's troops lost individual skirmishes, fell back, or were pulled back. Insofar as possible, Nasser directed the war from Cairo, and he soon became acutely aware of the failings of his armies. Far too often, though, he felt that information was being kept from him, and he decided one night to leave Cairo and go in person to Port Said to review defences in view of a possible attack there. At the time, many of his senior officers were convinced that the Allies would attack at Alexandria. Nevertheless, Nasser persisted, although he didn't get to Port Said that night. Sometime after midnight, he reached Ismailia. With him was Abdul Boghdadi, Minister of Rural and Municipal Affairs. The trip was not a pleasant one for either man, but Nasser in particular seemed unduly dispirited. In fact, he was "in a melancholy mood as again and again they drove past the wreckage of vehicles and tanks on the road, where they had been strafed by the unopposed Allied planes."[185] Nasser saw, first-hand, the results of the war, and lamented the loss of lives and equipment. Those with him felt that they "were watching a broken man."[186]

The confidence of the Egyptian defenders at Ismailia buoyed him somewhat, although they talked him out of going up the canal highway to Port Said. That road was not particularly good, even when I travelled on it, and it undoubtedly was much worse in November 1956. It would have been simply too dangerous for the country's president to be tramping around with minimal protection in Port Said, especially when an enemy attack was expected there. For that reason, Nasser stayed at Ismailia for what remained of the night. He went back to Cairo at dawn.

At about this time, he decided that if he was unable to prevent an invasion of his homeland, he could at least frustrate any enemy use of the Suez Canal. After promising the world that the canal would be kept open no matter what, he bowed to what he felt was now a tactical necessity and ordered the waterway closed.

In addition to the previously sunken ships blocking the harbour in Port Said, several other vessels were scuttled in various places along the canal as far south as the city of Suez. These comprised "twenty-seven ships, including tugs, dredgers, cement-laden barges, salvage vessels, a tank landing craft and floating cranes."[187] And because the scuttled craft were not all in one place, their presence caused a headache to foreign companies who used the canal. There were sixteen freighters in transit when the canal was closed. They had no way of getting out and were stuck there for months.

An ocean away in Washington, the war in Egypt, along with the ruthless Soviet suppression in Hungary, attracted much of the administration's attention, while the frenetic last rallies of the election campaign played themselves out before audiences that were both confused and concerned about world affairs. In general, the average American pays little attention to what happens outside his homeland. Yet in the dying days of the 1956 presidential election soul-searching, worried voters sought comfort in the familiar. They wanted a world at peace, and in increasing numbers they began to throw their support behind the man they thought could bring that about.

Shortly before election day, one newspaper sent reporters out across the nation to interview voters at random and to try to assess the mood of the country. "The prevalent theme among the voters they interviewed was that the crises overseas emphasized the need to keep in the White House the former five-star general who was the leader of the victorious allied troops in Europe in the Second World War." Then the paper added, "The impact of international events probably was greatest on a body of hitherto undecided voters — many of them supporters of Eisenhower four years ago — who, until now, had been contemplating a switch."[188] As we know, they stuck with Ike and re-elected him.

But the end of his first term and the beginning of his second were especially difficult. Eisenhower had to deal with the two major crises, but there was a frustrating lack of communication with London and Paris and the usual sabre-rattling by Nikita Khrushchev. With regard to the latter, the President was damned if he did, damned if he did not. If he sent American troops into Egypt to keep the peace, he faced the risk of Russian nuclear retaliation. If he did nothing, Russia could move into the Middle East and upset the global balance of power. In fact, there were many Soviet "technicians" already in Egypt, and there would be many more during the subsequent Aswan Dam construction.

On the other question involving France and Britain, the Americans were extremely frustrated: it seemed that both European countries had become closed-mouthed about their intentions and were barging ahead despite all the historical connections and alliances they had with Washington. Try as he might, Eisenhower seemed powerless to do much about what was happening.

Compounding the President's problems was the illness of John Foster Dulles. Eisenhower relied on Dulles, and indeed few decisions involving other countries were made unless they were vetted first by the Secretary of State. The President trusted Dulles, sought his advice, heeded his caution, and tolerated his excesses. No wonder, then, that his unexpected illness had the potential to cause a serious disruption in the nation's business, or at least in the foreign affairs business that impacted the Oval Office. Eisenhower leaned on Dulles so much that at times reporters' questions as to policy, protocol, and expectations were handed to Dulles when Ike was not sure of his footing. "Eisenhower set a framework, but within it Dulles's assiduous application, his talent for draftsmanship, his penchant for conceptual formulation and, above all, the trust which the President came to rest in his judgement made him a very powerful force."[189] That was why, even while the Secretary of State was recovering from a three-hour bowel operation to remove his cancer, important matters requiring urgent decisions were taken to him in his hospital room. Eisenhower ordered that Dulles was to be placed in the presidential suite at Walter Reed and even went to see him there. The President offered his best wishes for a complete recovery but then sought the sick man's advice on several government matters that were pending. "One of the items on the agenda was the wish of Eden and Mollet to come to Washington for a summit on Suez."[190] The visit did not happen, but the President wanted to discuss the matter with Dulles anyway.

Eisenhower appointed Herbert Hoover Jr., the Under Secretary of State, to replace the ailing Dulles, but because there was such a steep learning curve, the new man could not take over all the responsibility right away. Within days, Dulles "was receiving and reading important cables and speaking frequently with Hoover over the telephone and offering his advice to the President. Eisenhower was happy to receive it."[191]

But to a large degree, Dulles was already yesterday's man. The solving of the Suez crisis would now depend on other people in other places, and one of these places was Ottawa. It was there that Louis St. Laurent and his Cabinet met to work out the rough parameters of the peace proposal that Canada's Minister of External Affairs would take to the United Nations. Many of the details of the initiative were still undecided, but it would be up to Lester Pearson and his aides to work out as many of these as possible in the pressure-filled hours and minutes before he stepped to the podium in the General Assembly.

CHAPTER SIXTEEN

History at the United Nations

EVEN AS PRIME MINISTER Louis St. Laurent called his Cabinet to order in Ottawa on Saturday morning, November 3, 1956, worrisome moves were underway on "the wine-dark sea" between Malta and Cyprus and the coast of North Africa. The greatest naval armada since the Second World War assault on Hitler's Western Wall was steaming relentlessly towards its destination at the north end of the Suez Canal. Already, the unfortunate cities of Port Said and Port Fuad were reinforced as much as possible to withstand what looked to be inevitable. Anthony Eden's stubborn intent was coming to fruition. The air assault on Egypt was largely over; the one from the sea was about to begin.

In Ottawa, the men who assembled around the Cabinet table that morning knew they had little time. Pearson's plan was the only item they intended to deal with, and its consideration was more urgent, more global in its scope, and yet more undefined than almost any topic most who were there had ever considered. The meeting began at 10:00 a.m. and lasted a little over an hour, and Lester Pearson had the floor for most of the time. He was bleary-eyed, sleep-deprived, adrenaline-fuelled, and had already made several phone calls to London and Washington and held meetings in his office with the Egyptian ambassador, El Husseini El Khatib, and with Neil Pritchard, the Acting British High Commissioner to Canada.

Pearson brought his colleagues up to speed on what had happened at the UN and gave them a first-hand report on his abstention there and the reasons for it. He also filled in the details of developments in the U.K. and U.S. as he knew them that morning. There were several questions, comments, and suggestions made and considered, and then both the Prime Minister and the Minister of National Defence made their views known. "Mr. St. Laurent was encouraging," while Defence Minister Ralph Campney "was enthusiastic."[192] Both reactions were keenly satisfying for Pearson, who would, after all, be the one making the case for the Canadian plan at the UN. The fact that he had the unanimous backing of his colleagues made what he had to do less onerous. At least he did not have to worry about dissent within the ranks.

That originated elsewhere.

The *Globe and Mail*, arguably the most influential newspaper in the nation at the time, was barely on side. Most of its editorials were critical of Pearson's work and highly caustic because of his abstention in New York. It must have seemed to him at times that the *Globe* had half the information but all the answers. Had it been up to the editors of the paper, the Suez Crisis would have been solved much earlier, and they even had the temerity to say so. By abstaining from the vote at the UN, "the Canadian Government added nothing to its prestige — or to Canada's," the paper claimed. "External Affairs Minister Pearson did not actually cast Canada's vote against the Anglo-French effort to restore peace in the Middle East, but his abstention from voting had the same effect."[193] The paper supported the invasion.

Later in the same editorial, the *Globe* faulted Pearson for suggesting a UN force. "But why a UN police force? No such body exists, or has any prospect of coming into existence,"[194] the paper declared unequivocally. When a United Nations force actually was created — and quickly — the paper became slightly more reticent.

The discussion around the Cabinet table touched on several related matters concerning the establishment of the policing component. Pearson told the meeting that Britain and France had indicated that they would stop the war if some kind of policing organization stepped in. In what is called the Extract from Cabinet Conclusions for the day, there was an optimistic note concerning the acceptance of such an idea in New York. "If the U.K. and France would agree that the force should include detachments from other countries and all be landed under a UN military command, there was a good possibility that the General Assembly would give substantial support to such a plan."[195] Pearson

140

intended to do all in his power to make such a case as soon as he got back to New York. In the meantime, the Canadian Cabinet and most of the world hoped that fighting in Egypt would soon be curtailed for good. In the documents cited above, however, there was this cautionary note: "The chances of success would not be great, however, if the U.K. and France landed in strength and there was heavy fighting."[196]

Because that eventuality was about to come true, as Pearson feared it would, his immediate return to the United Nations was now critical. Just before adjourning that day, St. Laurent made reference to the fact that Parliament would have to be summoned in order to authorize the sending of Canadian troops to the Middle East if they were required. The ministers concurred, and the meeting ended.

After a hurried lunch, Pearson went over a last few details with the Prime Minister and then met with his own staff to flesh out the approach to be used in New York. There were, of course, so many imponderables that finalizing, or even attempting to finalize, matters became frustrating, time-consuming, and often impossible. And despite having some time during the afternoon to work on the logistics, Pearson knew that much had yet to be done. Nevertheless, all too soon, he had to get back to the UN.

"I left for New York at 5:00 p.m.," he recalled, "arriving at 6:45. I had, I remember, two or three press men with me on the plane who wanted to talk to me. All I wanted to do was look out the window and think about what I ought to do, how I ought to do it, and what the consequences would be."[197]

The atmosphere at the United Nations was electric that evening. Delegates and their staffs from all over the world met, agreed, disagreed, cajoled, and conversed about the forthcoming assembly session. There were meetings in every back room, lounge, and foyer, and hurried and insistent conversations continued at delegates' desks right up to the minute the meeting came to order. Pearson and the other Canadians who were there were involved, of necessity, in discussions concerning the momentous decisions that were to be made in the hours ahead. The matters to be considered were crucial, and it was felt that the Canadian plan should be made known to as many voting delegates as was possible before the formal session began. To this end, Pearson's people worked "among the senior advisers of the various delegations. In the lounge, in the corridors, interviews were going on, tactics decided, and quick decisions made. We worked quickly to get our resolution circulated informally that evening."[198] The idea was to give the delegates time to study the proposal before they had to react to it with their votes.

And study it they did. The great General Assembly building hummed with conversation, insistent lobbying, and barely concealed satisfaction from most delegates and their staffs that finally some resolution to the crisis in Egypt was in the wind. But there was not unanimity. At the same time as Eden's England seemed prepared to at least tolerate Pearson's suggestions for a resolution, the Australians, under Prime Minister Harold Menzies, were voicing their loud support for invasion. Not surprisingly, New Zealand concurred, and both nations made their views known to all who listened. Their efforts, however, went nowhere.

The three nations in Asia that were most vocal in their opposition to the Anglo-French-Israeli moves were India, Pakistan, and what was then Ceylon (now Sri Lanka). All were Commonwealth members, and all would continue to condemn the invasion because they feared it would lead to a wider war. They called it aggression and were adamant in their view that none of the three countries who had carried it out were justified in what they had done. India in particular looked at the attack on Egypt as a blatant violation of the charter of the United Nations.

Pearson and the rest of the Canadian contingent in New York knew the Asian point of view, and several times during those critical hours they listened to and learned from what India, Pakistan, and Ceylon were saying. Because Canada was a leading member of the Commonwealth, Pearson knew and for the most part had comfortable working relationships with delegates from these countries. Ultimately, "for once the United Nations abandoned posturing for peace-making, and the clearest reason was the work of Lester Pearson and the credit Canada had collected in a decade of middle-power diplomacy."[199]

But before the peacemaking became reality, the stage had to be set. Not only did the Canadian team work to ensure Britain, France, and Israel were on side — insofar as possible — they knew the views of Gamal Nasser had to be taken into account. It was, after all, his country that was literally under the gun. That was why Pearson had had his hurried meeting with the Egyptian ambassador prior to the Ottawa Cabinet meeting. Now, though, mainly through discreet and diplomatic approaches made to Nasser himself, the Canadian and American delegates in New York together learned that the Egyptian president was not adverse to the moves that were being made to counter the seaborne invasion that now threatened the Port Said–Port Fuad area.

By now, Henry Cabot Lodge, the American permanent representative at the UN, was in fairly constant contact with Pearson. The two men had been friends for years. Lodge might have had less clout in New York than the ailing Dulles, but he was better liked and easier to work with. And while Pearson rarely rated one diplomat over another, his working relationship with Lodge was a good one. The two men got together and decided what the opening move in the assembly should be. Both had motions written for public presentation, and after some comparison of details, the two concluded that the American wording was, as Pearson put it, "simpler."[200] For that reason, it was redrafted and worked into the Canadian approach. At this time, there was still some hope that the armada that was nearing the Egyptian coast could be somehow curtailed and that lives of both attackers and defenders might be spared. As always, innocent civilians who were in harm's way could be lost. That, to Pearson and everyone who worked on the resolution, would be the most unfortunate outcome of all. However, stopping the flotilla was not as easy as stopping a truck at a traffic light.

Many felt it could not be done — or at least, could not be done in time. For that reason, Selwyn Lloyd, the U.K. Foreign Secretary, was contacted by Norman Robertson in London. The Canadian High Commissioner sounded Lloyd out on the intended proposal in the General Assembly. Lloyd, and through him Eden, felt that they could support it, yet Lloyd "would not promise that there would not be landings."[201]

Years later, in his recollections of that time in his memoirs, Lloyd mentioned, "Our invasion fleet was sailing towards Port Said. Its speed was limited by the fact that the tank landing craft could only do five knots an hour." Then the retired minister added, rather ominously, "On 3rd November it was decided that the Minister of Defence should go ... to see whether the landing could be made sooner than planned."[202]

Those in New York knew they were working against the clock; they had to forge ahead and get the resolution on the floor as quickly as possible.

Finally, the last flurry of consultation complete, the Assembly opened at 8:00 p.m.; an Asian-African resolution was dealt with relatively quickly. Then Canada's Minister of External Affairs strode to the dais under the great seal of the United Nations and began to address the delegates before him. His speech was not a long one, but it was probably the most important he would ever give. Pearson talked at first about the general situation and the reason the particular session was being held. "The immediate purpose of our meeting tonight," he said, "is to bring about as soon as possible a cease-fire and a withdrawal of forces, in the area which we are considering, from contact and from conflict with each other."[203] He talked about the further implications of the motion he would make, but stressed the importance of the short-term intent. He then went directly to the core of his proposal, which asked the Secretary-General of the United Nations to prepare and submit to the General Assembly "within forty-eight hours a plan for the setting up, with the consent of the nations concerned, of an emergency international United Nations force to secure and supervise the cessation of hostilities."[204]

With those words, Pearson made history.

There was much discussion of the proposal, and then finally, sometime after 3:00 a.m., a roll call vote was held. The motion carried, with fifty-seven nations supporting it. No country cast a negative vote, but the Soviet Union, Britain, France, Australia, New Zealand, South Africa, Egypt, Israel, Laos, Portugal, and Austria all abstained.

The Canadians who were there that night were ecstatic, and the implications of what had been done were profound. As Pearson explained, "Although our resolution instructed the Secretary-General to report back within forty-eight hours, in fact a United Nations Emergency Force had been created. We did not put it exactly in those terms but that is what it meant."[205] And with peacekeepers in the field today, we are still acting on those few brief words expressed in New York that night in the late fall of 1956. Indeed, Canada has become a peacekeeping nation.

But following the vote, enormous hurdles had yet to be overcome. The most immediate were the ones that faced Dag Hammarskjöld. The sandy-haired, fifty-one-year-old Swiss civilian was a man of admirable restraint and quiet courage whose job now was to assemble an army in a couple of days. He must have wondered at the time if his US$20,000 salary per year plus US$35,000 expenses were worth it. However, as the son of a former Swedish prime minister and a member of his homeland's political elite, the tireless Secretary-General was as suited as anyone could have been for carrying out the mandate given to him.

Dwight Eisenhower admired Hammarskjöld and said of him: "The man's abilities have not only been proven, but a physical stamina that is almost unique in the world has also been demonstrated by this man, who, night after night, has gone with one or two hours' sleep — working all day, and, I must say, working intelligently and devotedly."[206] And now Hammarskjöld would work devotedly indeed. But first, he felt he had to do a closer assessment of what was required in the Canadian proposal. To that end, he called a meeting in his office in the late morning, not many hours after the General Assembly meeting concluded. Pearson was there. So were United Nations Under Secretary Ralph Bunche and a handful of others. The first organizational problem facing the group was the selection of the person who would lead the soon-to-be-created peacekeeping force.

For some time previously, the United Nations had had personnel in the Middle East who were part of what was called the Palestine Truce Supervision Organization, attempting to enforce the fragile Palestinian-Israeli peace. Their leader there was Lieutenant General E.L.M. "Tommy" Burns, a Canadian. Burns had had a praiseworthy career in both the First and Second World Wars, had been a deputy minister of Veterans Affairs in Ottawa, and had even been a part of the Canadian delegation to the United Nations in 1949. Hammarskjöld not only suggested to the group in his office that General Burns should lead the peacekeeping contingent in Egypt, he admitted that he had already contacted the general and had offered the job to him. Burns had accepted.

The men at the meeting now turned to the question of what countries should be asked to contribute troops to this instant army. From the outset, Canada was expected to be part of the contingent. In fact, Pearson had already indicated that when he addressed the General Assembly and introduced the idea of a police action. Now, he reaffirmed the commitment, provided that the inclusion of Canadians was approved by Ottawa and accepted by the United Nations itself. In fairly short order, the governments of Colombia, Sweden, Finland, Denmark, and Norway also indicated that they would contribute troops. Ultimately, India and Yugoslavia did as well.

But some nations were deliberately excluded. Britain and France both thought they should be part of the operation, but because they were already close to being branded aggressors, and because the Asian nations in particular would not accept Anglo-French troops in the role, neither was included. Initially, it was thought that the United States should be included, particularly as they had the necessary military hardware to cope with almost any eventuality. They also had large transport aircraft that could be used to ferry personnel anywhere they were needed. After additional consideration, however, the Americans were excluded, but for a different reason entirely: no one wanted the Russians involved. If the Americans were there, then in the Cold War climate of the time, the Soviets would also insist on being part of the force. Ultimately, all the big powers were excluded. The U.S. did ferry large numbers of troops from various countries to a staging area at Capodichino Airport at Naples, Italy, however. For political reasons, the soldiers were then taken from Italy to Egypt by Swissair. Finally, "less than a week after it came into existence, the United Nations Emergency Force had at its disposal some 5,000 troops of eight nations."[207]

There were, of course, innumerable teething problems for the instant army. Because of overcrowding at Capodichino, temporary billets had to be obtained. Food had to be trucked in. Weapons needed to be moved and secured. The soldiers themselves wore uniforms of their own countries, but it was felt that they should at least have distinctive helmets or berets. When not enough of the latter could be located quickly in either Europe or North America, the decision was made to use surplus United States Army helmets that happened to be stored at a military base at Leghorn, Italy. These were spray-painted UN blue and were distributed to the troops before they were flown to Egypt.

Before the meeting in Hammarskjöld's thirty-eighth-floor office wrapped up, he and Pearson reviewed the operation as they saw it, essentially "a two-stage process: first, a temporary force to supervise the ceasefire and withdrawal, and later, a second force to help maintain peace until a political settlement could be negotiated."[208]

Several other matters were identified and dealt with, the contribution of Canadian troops among them. Pearson phoned St. Laurent, who assured him that Canada would indeed be sending soldiers if required. That same night in Toronto, St. Laurent addressed the nation on radio and television and said Canadian soldiers would soon be going overseas again — not to fight a war, but, hopefully, to stop one.

CHAPTER SEVENTEEN

Ashore in Egypt

THE FORTY-EIGHT-HOUR PERIOD from the General Assembly vote until the report from the Secretary-General was due was a hectic one at the United Nations. It was a time of frantic, non-stop negotiation, organization, inter-government contact, and — for Pearson, Hammarskjöld, and those who worked with them — little sleep and unbelievable stress. "The advocates of emergency shirt-sleeve diplomacy kept exhaustion at bay with a continuing diet of sandwiches, coffee, Scotch, and aspirin,"[209] was the way one historian described the scene. In fact, "the lights that burned for the peacekeepers on the thirty-eighth floor [of the UN building] never went out during the days and nights of the race against the invasion fleet in the Mediterranean."[210] Yet, that being said, those most closely involved acquitted themselves admirably and did the bidding of the General Assembly by producing a report that was clear, cogent, and on time. But their efforts at times were extremely dispiriting.

The actions and decisions of Anthony Eden caused the most grief, largely because he believed he had to attack Egypt, no matter what world opinion might dictate. Hammarskjöld wrote to him and demanded that hostilities cease and that no amphibious landings be made. He reminded Eden that the UN was opposed to an invasion of Egypt and that an international force was being assembled to police the region. He also said that neither French nor British troops would be part of such a peacekeeping contingent.

But Eden refused to back down. On November 5, he wrote to St. Laurent and again made the case for Anglo-French intervention — even though the same day both the Israelis and the Egyptians had accepted a UN demand for a ceasefire, and Eden knew that. Nevertheless, in his top secret note to St. Laurent he said, "I should like you to know at once that … after discussion with the French; we have decided that the operation to separate the combatants and to ensure the safety of the canal must proceed as planned."[211] In other words, the attacks would go on regardless.

To be fair to the British, it must be pointed out that there was much disagreement in Eden's cabinet, as well as in the Labour Opposition and many of the newspapers, against going ahead with the seaborne assault. Eden's protégé in Parliament, Minister of State for Foreign Affairs Anthony Nutting, resigned over it, as did others. By this time, Eden had started to step back from the excuse of separating the combatants, because they were no longer fighting. He then claimed his principal reason for going ahead was to safeguard the canal. In fact, "he was so astonished by the speed with which the United Nations had reacted to Pearson's police force proposal that suddenly he was making it a condition for accepting a cease fire."[212]

Foreign Secretary Selwyn Lloyd was questioned in Parliament about his government's intentions in Egypt. In answer to an Opposition question he blurted out that Britain and France could not "ensure that the Israelis withdraw from the Egyptian territory until we are physically in the area to keep the peace."[213] In response, Labour Opposition parliamentarian Aneurin Bevan yelled back at Lloyd: "We have here not a military action to separate Israeli and Egyptian troops; we have a declaration of war against the Egyptian Government."[214]

And, in effect, that is what it was. In spite of the advice he received to the contrary, Eden decided that the seaborne attack should begin. It had already been preceded by the bombings and then the Anglo-French paratroop assault. However, in one last attempt to justify his actions insofar as Canada was concerned, Eden sent another top secret message to St. Laurent in Ottawa. In it, he claimed that he understood St. Laurent's misgivings but insisted that the Anglo-French force needed "to get there quickly and be on the ground." Then, referring to his own situation, he added that Britain had "incurred much criticism by the action we have been forced to take but I hope that you whose government have [sic] played a leading part in encouraging acceptance of the proposals for a United Nations force will regard what we have had to do as paving the way for it to become a reality."[215] The note was dated November 6, but was actually delivered to the Canadian prime minister at 9:15 p.m. on November 5. This was the night before the Anglo-French assault forces landed on the beach at Port Said.

Before dawn on November 6, the massive, slow-moving invasion force arrived off the North African coast. In the ships that were carrying them to war, thousands of young soldiers were awake and ready, wondering what the day would bring. They thought, for the most part, that the landing would be relatively easy, but at the same time they worried about their own safety. Not many of these men in uniform had ever been on a ship before, and after several days at sea they were anxious to get off, even if the land they expected to walk upon was a land at war. Many felt squeamish because they were not used to boats; in fact, some had hung over the rails so long, they had nothing in their stomachs anymore. A few were so seasick, they were sure they were dying. To them, falling on the field of battle could not be much worse — and it would bring more glory.

Some played cards, some tried to eat, some prayed, and some wondered what in hell they were doing here. The latter were a minority, however. Lots were sure Nasser was Hitler; he had taken the canal, and they intended to get it back. Most thought they would be doing that in short order. All were excited, some were scared — but they dared not admit it — and most wondered how they would perform under fire. To some of the older men, this was a bit like Normandy all over again.

Most of the troops were war ciphers who did what they were told. They obeyed orders, sometimes stupid and pointless orders, but they were soldiers, and that's what soldiers did. They sometimes liked their leaders, occasionally even respected them, but for the most part they regarded them as incompetent, glory hounds, egomaniacs, or tyrants. They rarely thought of their foul-mouthed, hot-tempered, narrow-minded sergeant as a man whose wife loved him, whose little children thought he was right next to God. Yet they would do what this bully demanded.

Then there were the officers. For the most part, they were older than the men they led. Most had more education, more military time, and more knowledge of where they were going that morning. Some had been to Egypt before. In fact, many had spent time there during the long occupation. More than a few had been to the Canal Zone, and even Port Said itself. Often they knew more about the place than the defenders they were going to shoot as soon as they landed. In fact, many of the Egyptian soldiers sent to defend Port Said were from Cairo, Alexandria, Suez, or any of the hundreds of nondescript villages that dotted the land. Most had never been to Port Said because there never had been a reason to go there.

But the officers on the ships that morning were often not sure what their orders were. They were hesitant and badly in need of a concrete set of expectations. That was in part because those at the highest echelons of the military were themselves not clear about what they were to do. And neither were those in charge of the whole operation.

That included Anthony Eden. The Prime Minister wanted his war, but, as some claimed, he didn't want to kill anybody. Most said he was a nice man but a weak leader and a bumbler. Whether they loved him or hated him, no one ever said he was cruel. For that reason, among others, Eden agonized over the thought of deaths in the attacks he had ordered. In particular, he dreaded the deaths of defenceless civilians. Even in his dispatches to his counterparts abroad, he mentioned this. One of these was Louis St. Laurent, who obviously had no control over how many civilians might be killed.

On November 5, for example, Eden assured St. Laurent that "in carrying out the operations no possible precaution will be spared to avoid civilian casualties and to reduce material damage to the absolute minimum. Adequate warnings will be broadcast to the civilian population concerned before military operations are launched."[216] And broadcasts were made. "For two hours before the assault 'The Voice of Britain' on Cyprus broadcast continuously warning people in Port Said to take cover."[217] But there were also other underlying reasons why the British government wanted few civilians harmed, "partly because of the pressure of world and domestic opinion and partly because of a desire to minimize inevitable Arab hostility towards Britain."[218] Eden knew, as did his ministers, that shelling a city was not going to please the people who lived there, nor would it please anyone else who regarded the residents as innocent victims in a struggle much larger than they.

As the first streaks of dawn illuminated the beachfront at Port Said, the city was at peace. The soldiers on the ships looked out, some in wonder, some in dread. They were going to fight a war, but neither they nor their senior officers knew exactly what kind of war it would be. That was because, up until the last minute, the big gun selection on board some of the main vessels had not been made.

During the night, Hugh Stockwell, the task force commander for the British and French ground forces, received a signal from London limiting the calibre of gun used in the bombardment. The restriction was intended to save civilian lives, and it was thought that Eden himself set the limits. The ruling stipulated that no gun with more than a 4.5-inch calibre could be used. The restriction automatically meant that the main batteries on the *Jean Bart*, the French battleship, could not be used, nor could the large guns on the cruisers in the armada. Finally, only minutes before shore bombardment was to begin, Stockwell was handed another revision in orders that had just come in a radio signal from London. This one called for the cancellation of the preliminary bombardment entirely.

The British general paced the deck of his headquarters ship, the *Tyne*, cursed the revision, and tried to decide what to do about it. Finally, because he was "reluctant to put his troops ashore without adequate fire support ... he accepted the London decision with respect to the naval bombardment, and cancelled it as ordered."[219] Instead, he decided to distinguish between naval bombardment and naval gunfire support. His troops would have the latter — and they did.

Meanwhile, in Port Said, the defending Egyptian troops were waiting, watching, and dreading what they knew was at hand. There were a couple of infantry battalions there, and they had with them a hodgepodge of guns, including anti-aircraft batteries that were intended for coastal defence. And after his visit to Ismailia on the previous night, Nasser had sent additional troops to Port Said, among them three National Guard contingents. Also, in a move that was somewhat unusual at the time, he had a large number of small arms of various sorts sent to the city by train. These were handed out to individual citizens, with the exhortation that they use them to defend their homeland. In the days to come, a certain number were used against the attackers, but just as often, those who received them kept them for personal protection against looters — most of whom were roving bands of Egyptian gangs intent on using the chaos around them to further their own ends.

153

Within a couple of days, shopkeepers who got the guns were more interested in setting them aside to bargain with the young soldiers who suddenly were everywhere in the downtown core. Nasser also directed that
three or four large self-propelled guns be brought from the Sinai.

The hours immediately prior to the opening salvos from offshore were
eerily quiet in both Port Said and Port Fuad. Citizens remained indoors,
protected themselves as best they could, and closed every window and
door to the outside. As the morning wore on, the streets remained desert-
ed. Shops were closed, and the iron grills on the storefronts remained
down and secured. Indeed, the twin towns were preparing for siege.

The first phase of the fighting was not from the ships offshore but
from attack aircraft out of Cyprus that flew in low, fast, and with dead-
ly effect. They strafed the beach area to the north of Port Said and
destroyed several of the smaller buildings there, signalling to the
Egyptian defenders something of what was to follow. In doing so, they
also convinced many of the dug-in troops to clear out and scurry to
more secure defences among the labyrinth of small streets, cul-de-sacs,
and rabbit warren structures that were part of the city behind them.

No sooner was the air strafing over than the guns from the
destroyers opened up in a deliberate attempt to soften the resistance
the attacking troops might face. The barrage from the sea did not
include the largest guns, but it did destroy several buildings adjacent
to the beach and harbour area. As well, two large circular oil storage
tanks were hit. They immediately started to burn, and clouds of dense,
black, acrid smoke drifted over the landscape and occasionally wafted
out to sea as the wind shifted. These fires burned for some days and,
coupled with the building fires, often obscured parts of the city as the
attacking forces arrived.

While the navy shelling was going on, preparations for amphibious
landings were being finalized. Royal Marine commandos climbed into the
Landing Vehicles Tracked, or "Buffaloes," and, as soon as conditions permitted, ploughed towards the beach. They were followed throughout the
day by men and machines in other landing craft. Gradually, the increasing number of attackers took control of Port Said. Over in Port Fuad, the
landing went well also, but the French troops coming ashore there faced
relatively little resistance. Port Said was a tougher town to conquer.

Interestingly, the assault on Port Said was the first time helicopters were used by attackers in war. (They were used for medevac purposes in Korea.) By today's standards, the twenty-two Royal Navy and Royal Air Force choppers used were small, uncomfortable, and decidedly primitive. The green-painted machines were called either Whirlwinds or Sycamores. The latter carried only three passengers, who had to sit on the floor with two of the three hanging their legs outside. The men in the Whirlwinds had "no seats, doors or windows and precious few hand-holds. Communication between the pilot and his passengers ...was effected by shouts or by ... tugging at the pilot's legs."[220] Nevertheless, the helicopters served their purpose and successfully carried troops from the ships to the beach area along the canal mouth, near the then intact statue of Ferdinand de Lesseps. They also evacuated wounded soldiers, British and French — and Egyptian. These casualties were treated on a hospital ship. Through the whole endeavour, only one helicopter was lost. Fortunately, the pilot and the three wounded men he carried were all plucked from the sea.

As the day wore on, the Egyptian defenders were pushed back. The numbers of attackers mushroomed, and they gradually got more equipment offloaded. Of particular help were several tanks, which, when faced with pockets of resistance, were able to blast their way forward and speed up the advance.

Then, in late morning, an unexpected development occurred. A signal, ostensibly from the American consul in Port Said, reported that the Egyptian commandant had apparently assessed the way the fighting was going and decided to surrender his city to the Anglo-French command. The rather cryptic message reached General Stockwell on the headquarters ship *Tyne*, and he in turn contacted his second-in-command, General Beaufre, who was on anther vessel, the *Gustave-Zede*. The report stated that the surrender would take place in the Suez Canal Company offices in the inner harbour at Port Said. Accordingly, Beaufre went over to the *Tyne*, where the two generals and a couple of other senior officers embarked on a ship's launch and headed into the city. Fighting was still going on on either side of them, and the launch also had to avoid the scuttled ships that blocked the canal.

The little boat, now followed by a second craft with several newspaper reporters, moved slowly through the outer harbour, past the shell-blasted police station on the starboard side, and gradually eased closer to the Canal Company offices. Then, as Beaufre himself put it later, "at a range of 100 yards, we were greeted by a hail of bullets, some of which hit the launch. If someone was waiting for us at the Canal Company building, surrender was clearly not his purpose."[221]

Needless to say, the sailor at the wheel did a frantic about-turn and beat a hasty retreat. Had the Egyptians who fired from the building waited another five minutes, they could have captured the two senior soldiers who were running the Allied side of the war. Fortunately for those on the launch, no one was hurt in the enfilade.

The *Tyne* launch returned to the outer harbour where, rather surprisingly, both Stockwell and Beaufre decided to get off — Stockwell on the Port Said side of the canal and Beaufre across at Port Fuad. Ostensibly, they wanted to assess the progress of the attacks on the two cities and visit their own troops who were there. Later on, the two were faulted for their actions, partly because they had placed themselves in danger, but even more so because neither was in a position to respond to directives from London. One historian, writing fairly recently, mentioned that Stockwell "wandered around Port Said until well after nightfall. His decision to spend the day incommunicado rather than on board the *Tyne*, where updates from his superiors and situation reports were available, remains inexplicable. Beaufre made a similarly unfathomable choice. He lingered in the French zone, talking to French commanders at Port Fuad and preparing for subsequent Canal Zone operations."[222]

Stockwell and his deputy had made themselves unavailable when important decisions regarding the war were being made elsewhere. And those decisions had now reached a critical point.

CHAPTER EIGHTEEN
The End of the War

WHILE THE NEWSPAPERS OF THE WORLD were covering the progress of the war in Egypt, real advances were being made to end it. The race against time at the United Nations in New York was beginning to bear fruit. After the decision had been made to create the United Nations Emergency Force (UNEF), Dag Hammarskjöld, Lester Pearson, and other senior officials worked flat out to draft the report on the formation of the peacekeeping body. The time passed in the twinkling of an eye, but finally, at about two o'clock in the morning on November 6, the document was ready for presentation to the General Assembly. By then, though, the Anglo-French Allies were storming the beaches at Port Said.

In the forty-eight hours during which the UNEF protocol was being prepared, several other related developments had occurred. The Soviets made their position known in letters to England, France, and Israel, claiming that "Russia was ready to crush them, by use of 'every kind of modern weapon.'"[223] Even though the note implied the use of nuclear weapons, all three countries receiving the threats felt they were best ignored. At the same time, Russia stated that both it and the United States might go into Egypt and "separate the combatants." As expected, Dwight Eisenhower dismissed this suggestion out of hand. To him, there were enough Russian "advisers" there already.

In England, Anthony Eden had endured much recrimination because of his stance on the war and his determination to land troops in the Canal Zone when there was no real reason to do so. The Israel-Egypt fight was over — and the Israel side of it had been pre-arranged anyway.

Nevertheless, the more Eden charged ahead, the louder his critics became, until eventually he must have thought his entire world was against him.

Then his health, which had long been precarious, took a decided downturn. His irritability increased, his patience evaporated, and his judgment was being called into question by even his friends. Yet he continued to lead his land as best he could; while UNEF was being set up, and before a ceasefire came out of New York, he was determined that his troops should gain and hold as much territory in Egypt as they possibly could. He applauded their efforts on the day of the landings.

But while the Port Said war was relatively brief, it was both destructive and brutal. This was particularly so for those unfortunate civilians who suffered and died through no fault of their own. They were the tragic victims in a military campaign they neither wanted nor understood. Their homes and shops were often levelled, their jobs disappeared, and their city was shattered — but most of all, lives were lost: family members, friends, and neighbours were suddenly no longer there.

At the time the battle for Port Said began, there were an estimated eight hundred British civilians living there,[224] but it was the Egyptian poor who died most often. "They arrived in trucks, hearses, ambulances and even a Coca-Cola lorry," wrote a young medical doctor from Britain. "Loads and loads of bodies, of all ages, and both sexes. They were buried in roughly bulldozed mass graves."[225]

Others reported similar situations. *Time* magazine correspondent Frank White went to a hospital in Port Said in order to understand first-hand what the war meant to the local people. "In normal times," he told his editors in New York, "the Egyptian General Hospital can take care of forty patients in each of its eight wards. When I visited it had no light, no water, no food and no medical supplies." The chief surgeon related that in the two days of fighting, there had been over five hundred deaths there and that "at one point corpses were piled nearly as high as a man's head in three sheds and covered the entire back lawn of the hospital."[226]

But in London and Paris, politicians who favoured the war told their constituents that there were few deaths among the invading forces and that they in turn had targeted military objectives only. Insofar as possible, they said, civilians were spared, and so was their property.

Little was said of civilians who attempted to fight back. One of these was a young man who was as brave as he was naive.

He had been one of those given a rifle after Nasser's supply train came in. Because he had never had such a weapon before, he apparently believed he was invincible with it in his hands. He even believed it was powerful enough to stop a tank. His brother later explained what happened when the young man encountered one of the machines rumbling through Port Said: "He stood in the middle of the street, rifle in hand. The tank kept approaching nearer and nearer until [it] was as close as a single step. He then fired his rifle believing that he will hit the tank, but before hearing the sound of his shot my brother was a heap of flesh underneath the tank."[227]

And he was not the only one who died tragically. There is documentary evidence of French paratroops shooting unarmed Egyptian fishermen they took prisoner at Lake Manzala. The fisherman stood in their boats, protested their innocence, and begged for mercy. Because the soldiers did not want the bother of looking after any prisoners, they simply shot them. As one of the paratroops, Pierre Leulliette, admitted later, "No useless prisoners! We emptied our magazines. And one after the other the prisoners fall." Two of the Egyptians dived into the water and desperately attempted to swim to safety. Sadly, they did not succeed. As soon as they came up to catch their breath, they were shot. "And the head disappears," Leulliette continued, "mangled, blasted, at point-blank range. The second head comes out of the water a little further off, with close-cropped hair like the first and the same wide-open, terror-stricken eyes, and it shares the same fate."[228]

As a result of the shelling of Port Said and the advance southward, the town was considerably damaged. Along with many office buildings and businesses, entire apartment blocks were reduced to rubble. Dust, smoke, and the stifling stench of acrid chemicals seemed to permeate everything. Buildings were ablaze, as were rows of palm trees. The sound of screaming and the smell of death hung in the air, and the noise of the battle was pervasive.

There was fighting at the police station, but eventually, it fell to the British. All the while, "Egyptian forces engaged in a fighting retreat — slow, organized withdrawal in the face of superior firepower."[229] The fighting then jumped from the heavily fortified police station to the

Suez Canal Company offices, where the two Allied generals had come under fire earlier. Now, the building was on fire after having been hit by the guns of the tanks. Fortunately, the flames were doused, the beautiful old structure was saved, and it came under British control. Then the soldiers went on "in small groups, keeping close to buildings, the men doubled across road intersections jumping or stepping over bodies, debris and piles of boxes of Czech self-loading rifles, most of them empty but a few still intact. They were little hindered by the shooting which seemed to be going on all around them."[230]

WHILE ALL THIS WAS HAPPENING IN EGYPT, the UN peacekeeping paper was being introduced in New York. The General Assembly hall was packed for the presentation, and at the close of it, a ceasefire in Egypt was proposed and agreed upon. The forces at war were to stop fighting at midnight GMT on November 6. This meant that the ceasefire in Egypt was at 2:00 a.m. on November 7. The media spread the word, while the official notification was passed along to the senior army commanders as soon as they could be reached. They were already planning operations for the following day, in which paratroop landings would take place at Qantara and Ismailia, since the military objective was to bring as much of the Canal Zone as they could under Allied control as quickly as possible. However, neither objective became reality. Apart from scattered last-minute skirmishes, the Suez war was over. Allied troops controlled Port Said and Port Fuad and had advanced twenty miles or so south along the canal to the village of Al Cap. There they set up a makeshift guard post and waited for further orders.

In the two cities, there was an immediate attempt to restore a measure of law and order, but this was not always easy. The local people and the Egyptian soldiers who had been fighting there naturally looked upon the British and the French, not just as interlopers, but as enemies. Peace might have come in theory, but the foreign troops who walked the streets with guns were both despised and feared. After all, until they had been told to stop fighting, they were there to wage war. Just because they were suddenly peacemakers did not mean they were welcome.

Here and there in Port Said, Egyptian snipers made life unpleasant for the Allies on the streets. Men hidden in upper rooms holding Czech rifles occasionally took potshots at the foreigners, but for the most part there were no widespread insurrections or killings. Gradually, a measure of calm became the norm, and from then on, most of the news out of Egypt dealt with peacekeeping. But before that came about, there were some who were actually upset because the war was over. This point of view was most often voiced by soldiers who had come so far to fight and then barely had a chance to do so. In some cases, troop ships had yet to unload.

French paratrooper Pierre Leulliette claimed that because peace and then withdrawal from Egypt came so quickly, he and his fellow soldiers had to "stomach the shame, the ridicule, the ignominy of retreating as if disgracefully beaten, after we had won."[231] One of his counterparts in the British army, Sandy Cavanagh, felt that the abruptly ended war "had been a futile and expensive waste of time."[232] He neglected to mention that it was also a tragic waste of lives and resources.

Even Andre Beaufre, the officer commanding the French forces, was disillusioned, so it is probably no surprise that the troops under him felt the same way. On the night the war ended, the general was eating dinner on the *Gustave-Zede* when "an officer came to report that a BBC broadcast heard in the wardroom had announced that the French and British governments were ordering the cease fire." As soon as he realized the implications of that decision, as he recalled, "the news hit me like a blow in the pit of the stomach."[233] The French officer wrote extensively about Suez in the years that followed. He always regarded it as a defeat — one brought about by several factors, but, nonetheless, a defeat.

In England, the Prime Minister was in for a difficult time. He had dithered, procrastinated, and, worst of all, shown a lack of leadership that was unforgivable. "In the country at large, Eden's position was not unnaturally considered to be at risk. The Suez policy had been very personally connected with the Prime Minister and its execution had notoriously and to an unusual degree centered on him."[234] While the country was at war and the troops were on the ground and fighting and dying for a cause, most Britons had held their tongues. Now, however, the Suez policy was being questioned as never before, and "although true believers went on talking about its success, everybody else seemed convinced that it was a most total failure."[235] As far as Eden was concerned, when he'd pushed the nation into war, he'd had two main objectives: to take back the canal and, if possible, to topple Nasser. Neither happened, so judged against those objectives, the war was a failure. Publicly, Eden claimed to have wanted the Egyptians and the Israelis to stop fighting. They did, but he didn't. Or at least, not until he was forced to.

Everywhere, the talk turned, not to the fall of Port Said, but to the fall of Anthony Eden. He had committed thousands of men, extensive military hardware, and the resources of his nation to his war, and at the end, he had little to show for it but failing health and a ruined reputation. In Parliament, he was pilloried. In the press, criticized. In his own circle, pitied. Those closest to him knew he was a sick man; those farther away didn't care.

In America, Dwight Eisenhower, re-elected and secure in the Oval Office, took Eden's phone call and agreed with his wish to come for a visit to Washington. However, after conferring with his aides and others, including the hospitalized Dulles, he phoned back and told Eden not to come. America did not want to be seen, even by implication, as having supported the Suez debacle. Indeed, to a great extent, it was pressure from the United States that brought an end to the whole sorry venture.

There was also a looming financial crisis that fall, and that got Harold Macmillan's attention. The Chancellor of the Exchequer realized that Britain was going to need help, and quickly, in order to save its faltering economy. He also realized that the only country able to provide substantial monetary assistance was the United States. Understandably, America had no intention of helping if Britain was going to continue to waste resources in a war that might continue indefinitely — for that matter, on a war that Washington had opposed from the outset. In effect, the Eisenhower administration was telling Eden to cut and run in Egypt or to forget about getting bailed out. In time, the Prime Minister had no choice but to accept.

While all of these matters were going on elsewhere in the world, the outward serenity in Ottawa was somewhat misleading. As soon as the decision was made to establish UNEF, increased pressure fell on the Canadian government to respond — in terms of leadership, soldier selection, deployment of troops, provision of equipment, transportation overseas, and food and accommodation for those who were sent abroad. There were hundreds of items that had to be addressed between agreeing to contribute and getting those selected to wherever they were needed most. What our soldiers would actually do in the field had yet to be clarified.

As soon as he was able to do so after the UN General Assembly decision in New York, Pearson phoned Cabinet Secretary R.B. Bryce in Ottawa and confirmed that Hammarskjöld was asking for several countries to provide troops for the United Nations force, and that Canada was among them. In all, the Secretary-General envisioned a force of about ten thousand, which meant Ottawa would be tasked with selecting and providing about a tenth of that number. These officers and men would have to be selected right away, if possible within two weeks. Already, a Polish contingent had offered its services, but because that country was then a Soviet satellite, hasty moves to counteract any Communist involvement were necessary. Should they have been included, the Poles would have received direction from Moscow, and that was no more desirable than having Washington calling the shots for any other group of participants in the field.

The call from Pearson was acted upon immediately, and Defence Minister Ralph Campney called an urgent meeting in his Parliament Hill office to decide what to do first. The next morning, when the Cabinet came together, he announced his intentions. Unfortunately, the first decision he made was a bad one, and in the days that followed, it would cause Pearson and Hammarskjöld no end of grief. It would also be a major embarrassment to Canada.

CHAPTER NINETEEN

The Wrong Regiment

THE FEDERAL CABINET met for three hours on the morning of November 7. However, before the ministers got down to the business at hand, Prime Minister Louis St. Laurent reported on a telephone conversation he had just had with Dwight Eisenhower, the newly re-elected President of the United States. The two men had talked for some minutes, and because they knew and respected each other, the discussion was friendly. St. Laurent congratulated Eisenhower on his electoral victory and then received congratulations in return. As reported by St. Laurent, Eisenhower mentioned that "he did not know of any government that had acted more admirably in the present crises than had that of Canada."[236] The men around the Cabinet table that day received this information with satisfaction, and it stiffened their resolve to continue to deal with Middle East matters in the best way they knew. The press and public might fault them, but as always, support from the President of the United States was appreciated. The previous few weeks had been difficult ones for Canada, particularly with regard to the public split with Britain and France over Suez.

The first item of formal business at the meeting dealt in rather general terms with Dag Hammarskjöld's request for troops who would be part of the peacekeeping force in the Middle East. The Minister of National Defence "proposed to provide a battalion group, augmented by supporting service troops, totalling approximately 1,000 to 1,500 men." He went on to say that these soldiers could be flown into the staging area close to where they would be needed, and then the aircraft carrier HMCS *Magnificent* "would be able to go to the Mediterranean in two or three weeks time loaded with supplies and equipment."[237] Further discussion followed, most of which dealt with the question of parliamentary approval for the undertaking, the monetary factors, and the wording and timing of press releases detailing the government's approach. The meeting concluded after the Prime Minister apprised everyone of his ongoing telephone conversations with Lester Pearson, who was still in New York. The UN was now debating exactly how and when the British and French troops presently in the Port Said area would be withdrawn. Pearson, who had been in regular attendance at the sessions, had indicated that he would keep his colleagues in Cabinet informed of developments as they occurred.

Reaction from the Canadian public was generally relief that the war was over. This was particularly true for those — and there were many — who had feared that the hostilities in the Middle East might spread and result in another world war. But there were some, and I remember them from my university days, who wanted the conflict to continue. They were convinced that had it done so, Canada would have been dragged into it and they would have been in uniform. Secretly, I felt then, and I feel now, that they just wanted to become heroes or officers, preferably both. But in my judgment, those who wanted war would have been the worst kind of leaders imaginable.

Letters to the editor in most Canadian papers reflected the usual variety of reactions about the ceasefire. As expected, while the *Globe and Mail* grudgingly accepted the UN accord, their editorials continued to champion the actions of Britain and France. On November 9, the lead editorial decried the Soviet brutality in Hungary and rather disparagingly played down the United Nations resolve in the Middle East. The paper indicated that it was still accepting at face value the Anglo-French excuse for going to war in the first place. Now, with the cessation of hostilities, the paper was almost sarcastic in its interpretation of the ceasefire: "So much for the British and French intervention in the Middle East — an intervention aimed at stopping a war between Israel and Egypt, and protecting the Suez Canal."[238] The paper was loath to admit that Israel and Egypt had stopped fighting before the intervention even began. In yet another editorial three days later, the editors mentioned that the *New York Times* felt that the Anglo-French intervention in Egypt had been unwise. Never one to concede a point, however, the *Globe* stuck to its guns: "This newspaper emphatically disagrees. There have been great losses, yes; but there have been greater gains. Future historians will, we believe, applaud rather than condemn the British and French action."[239]

The paper ran a number of negative letters that accused the federal government of being too American, anti-British, and even anti-Canadian. On November 9, two Toronto correspondents penned a joint note in which they covered all three bases: "We are not surprised at Mr. St. Laurent and his Liberal American lapdogs following at the heels of their American masters. It should be apparent even to the sleepiest Canadians that they have conspired in every way to sell out Canadian interests to the U.S." Then the writers added that they were concerned that "the Liberals have planned a separation from Britain and they possibly feel that this is the opportune time to bring it out into the open." The correspondents saved their best for last, adding an appeal they surely must have thought was overdue: "We feel that it's about time the Canadian people faced the facts of the Liberal Party's patently treasonous and insidiously dictatorial and generally anti-democratic, anti-British and anti-Canadian policies."[240]

Other publications and other commentators reacted in a variety of ways. The well-respected and eminent political observer Blair Fraser pointed out that high-level Canadian government spokesmen had always felt that "the idea of responding with military force to Colonel Nasser's seizure of the canal company sounded like sheer hysteria."[241]

In the same piece, however, Fraser noted that "Canadian popularity in London and Paris has been sharply depleted by the argument over the Suez Canal." He admitted having been "startled by the bitterness and ferocity among normally reasonable people,"[242] who felt Canada let its mother countries down by not rushing to their aid.

In a conversation with Fraser a few years later in Ottawa, he told me that in his opinion, the reputation of Canada was greatly enhanced because we did not go to war, compared to what it might have been had we gone to the aid of the combatants when the assault on Egypt took place.

Now we *were* going to provide aid to Britain and France, but this aid was more of a bailout from the untenable position in which they found themselves. Canada would be sending troops, not to fight, but to prevent fighting. The soldiers chosen to go on the peacekeeping mission were members of the Queen's Own Rifles.

The Queen's Own, as they were generally called, was an old and proud military regiment in Canada. It was organized in Toronto in 1860 and had been an integral part of the most important campaigns Canadians fought in since that time. Members served in every war from the Boer to Korea and lost hundreds of men in the process. Three Victoria Cross winners were Queen's Own soldiers. In November 1956, the regiment was composed of three battalions — a militia unit in Toronto, a second battalion in Victoria, and a third in Calgary. It was the Calgary contingent that was chosen to go to Egypt, and its members were pleased to have been selected for the job.

Under the leadership of forty-year-old Lieutenant-Colonel Clifford P. McPherson, the men had retained most of their fighting form in the three years since the Korean armistice had been signed. The troops looked upon their commanding officer as a soldier's soldier and were aware that he had been wounded while serving with the Cape Breton Highlanders during the Second World War. Now, he had to get his men ready for a different kind of job, in a faraway land, in less than two weeks. He assured his superiors that he was up to the task, and within minutes of having it handed to him, he began to carry it out. Little did he know at the time that his efforts would be for naught. Nevertheless, he succeeded in getting his soldiers ready to go within the time allocated. They were flown in flying boxcar aircraft to Halifax.

While these developments were underway in Canada, the UN delegates in New York squabbled about advisory committees, countries to be included in the peacekeeping force, cession of territory, clearing of the canal, and a host of other, seemingly unsolvable problems. But things did get done.

Yet even popular decisions had teething problems. In his new role as commander of the peacekeepers, Canadian General Tommy Burns flew to New York and spent many hours conferring with Hammarskjöld, Pearson, other UN officials, as well as with representatives of the countries who would be contributing to his force. Because he had led the earlier truce supervision team in the Middle East, he had in place a handful of senior officers whom he retained for UNEF. For the most part, Burns was respected by both the Israelis and the Egyptians, even though they had disagreed with some of his decisions in his previous role. Now that he would be the boss of the new peacekeeping force, it seemed that both sides were prepared to accept him — albeit somewhat grudgingly. Both knew that his appointment was logical, given the pressing time constraints under which it was made.

But almost immediately, problems arose from both countries. The Israelis refused categorically to have peacekeeping troops on their soil. As Pearson would write later, in a tone of resignation: "This was disappointing but not unexpected."[243] The stumbling block did make Hammarskjöld's job much more complicated and arduous than it might otherwise have been. However, because it was in the Canal Zone that peacekeepers were needed quickly, Hammarskjöld felt he could live with the Israeli obduracy.

Then the Egyptians had a complaint. Shortly after 7:00 p.m. on Sunday, November 11, Pearson was in his room at the Drake Hotel when the phone rang. The caller was Doctor Omar Loutfi, who at the time was the permanent representative for Egypt at the United Nations. Pearson knew him well and readily agreed when Loutfi asked if he could stop by the hotel because he wanted to talk in confidence about a "delicate matter." A few minutes later, he tapped on Pearson's door.

After some preliminary small talk, the obviously embarrassed Egyptian diplomat eased into an explanation for his being there. "He said that his government had accepted the idea of the international force and they were very appreciative of the role which had been played by Mr. Pearson and by Canada in the present crisis. They were very anxious to have General Burns, a Canadian, in charge of the international force. There was a problem, however, about Canadian troops."[244]

Pearson asked what was the matter with Canadian troops — but in his heart, knew what was coming. In fact, he had anticipated the problem, and later referred to it in his memoirs: "I knew that we were going to have some difficulties from the moment I received a telephone message at the Assembly that what Ottawa had in mind for UNEF was the Queen's Own Rifles."[245] Pearson realized that because British soldiers had been based in Egypt for seventy-four years, and had only ended their occupation there a little over two years earlier, it was rather obvious that they certainly would not be welcomed back. During much of the time in occupation, they were known as the Soldiers of the Queen.

"Yet here we are," Pearson continued, "sending the Queen's Own, wearing essentially a British uniform with UN badges. The Egyptians had just been fighting the Queen's Own."[246]

In his answer to Pearson's question, the Egyptian said that while Nasser and the nation were agreeable to UNEF being on Egyptian territory, they did not want Canadians there.

Pearson was furious, and he made sure his visitor knew it. He explained to Loutfi that Canada had led the initiative for the forming of UNEF, that the Canadian government agreed with the move, that the people of Canada supported the idea, and that it was preposterous for a Canadian general to be leading troops of several nations but not to be allowed to lead his own.

Loutfi quickly excused himself and left, but before going, he agreed to relay the Canadian reaction to his superiors. The next day, Hammarskjöld flew to Cairo and discussed what had happened with President Nasser himself. Still later, General Burns "discreetly informed Ottawa that his real need was for competent administrative troops. In due course, HMCS *Magnificent* left for Egypt laden with vehicles, equipment, supplies, and most of a thousand-man contingent from the supporting arms and services. The Queen's Own went back to Calgary."[247] Much later in their peacekeeping tenure, Canadian soldiers of various regiments were deemed acceptable to Egypt.

But during Hammarskjöld's visit with Nasser, the Secretary-General found himself agreeing — unwisely, as it turned out — to accept the condition that UNEF would remain in Egypt only as long as Nasser himself permitted. Several years hence, this point in the peacekeeping agreement would cause real problems. Yet in early November 1956, getting UNEF troops on the ground as quickly as possible was paramount.

Lester Pearson's work during this period was full of constant frustration. He laboured diligently, both in New York and Ottawa, and at times it seemed as if he lived on airplanes. However, apart from his angry remarks to Loutfi at the Drake that night, there was really only one show of temper. It also had to do with the Queen's Own selection, but on that occasion, Pearson bit his tongue and declined to express what was really on his mind. The matter came to a head during a telephone conversation with the bull-headed and volatile Ralph Campney, who had made the call to Pearson in New York to tell him of the selection of the Queen's Own. Pearson could not believe the insensitivity of the choice and attempted to object. However, as he admitted later, "when I voiced my misgivings to our Minister of National Defence, his reaction was so immediate and violent that I did not pursue the subject."[248]

In contrast to Campney's serious blunder, the work done by Pearson was both effective and sound. He handled issue after issue adroitly and with aplomb — and, as he probably would have admitted, with a lot of luck on his side. Being able to work effectively with Hammarskjöld was also a bonus. Even though the Secretary-General laboured unceasingly through those critical days, it was because he was "wholeheartedly behind the fulfillment of Lester Pearson's idea."[249] Pearson, in turn, lauded Hammarskjöld.

In Britain, Anthony Nutting, the minister of state who resigned rather than support Anthony Eden over Suez, wrote of the futility of going to war and the effects of the decision as they pertained to Britain. At that difficult time it was Pearson, Nutting explained in a later account, who "had thrown us a straw and we were clutching at it in a desperate attempt to extricate ourselves from our predicament."[250] As far as we know today, such praise was heartfelt.

It was reflected by what others said as well. A reporter for a British newspaper wrote of Pearson's work and his attempts to nail down concrete results in an atmosphere of crisis at the United Nations. "The Canadians, with the international prestige won by the fecundity of Mr. Pearson's imagination and the objectivity of their behaviour in similar situations, seemed to promise a more satisfactory solution than has been achieved before."[251]

A couple of days later, a former British Home Secretary who was visiting Canada made a speech in Toronto praising the work being done by this country to alleviate the situation in Egypt. J. Chester Ede told his audience, "Canada's prestige in world councils has been greatly advanced by her actions in the Middle East crisis."[252] But the same issue of the paper that reported on Ede's address carried a letter to the editor from Charles A. Wunder of Toronto, who had a different opinion.

"Apparently Papa St. Laurent and Lester Pearson would rather clear all their thinking with Washington before they can make up their minds where they stand," wrote Wunder, and then added rather forcefully, "I for one think our proper place is with England and not with this atheistic UN."[253] It is doubtful if Ede would have felt the same way about the United Nations. He had been in the city to address the International Association for Liberal Christianity and Religious Freedom.

Meanwhile, in Halifax, the Queen's Own were about to return to Calgary, and the people of Halifax were sorry to see them go. The local paper commented on the matter, noting that "Nova Scotia in general and Halifax in particular have been glad to have the Queen's Own Rifles in their midst." According to the paper, "Halifax shares the regret of the unit that their visit here is not now to be crowned by service overseas, but with that regret is mingled a very real pleasure that we have had the opportunity of entertaining them as visitors."[254]

There had been little time for either socializing or sightseeing, but they had made time for some of both, and as they departed Halifax the men from the west would remember a beautiful port town instead of their peacekeeping adventure that never was. Their exclusion from UNEF was about to become a topic of lively debate and contention in Parliament and across the country.

CHAPTER TWENTY

Canadians Arrive in Egypt

IN THE FALL OF 1956, Howard Green was a member of the Official Opposition in the Government of Canada. Some two and a half years later, he would become the Minister of External Affairs under John Diefenbaker. He was always a staunch anglophile and supporter of the Commonwealth and for those reasons was extremely critical of the role played by Lester Pearson during the Suez Crisis. He had convinced himself, and subsequently did all he could to convince other Canadians, that Pearson had committed the most serious of sins because he did not support Britain in its hour of need. He became one of Pearson's worst enemies over the matter.

And as we noted earlier, he was not alone. Even as the three troop trains were taking the 950 officers and men of the Queen's Own from Halifax to Calgary, even as the maintenance, support, and communications personnel were leaving for Egypt, the debate over Canada's failure to support Britain continued to rage. Nevertheless, it was Green, "a political opportunist masquerading as a non-drinking messianic peacemaker,"[255] who led the charge. He loudly proclaimed that the creation of UNEF cast aspersions on the good name of Canada and that St. Laurent and Pearson had hurt Britain. Later on, when he became a member of the governing Conservatives, he "eventually came to believe that humanity was in such peril that only he and Canada could lead the way to peace."[256] He was undoubtedly jealous of Pearson and his Nobel Prize, and he apparently sought the award for himself.[257]

In the fall of 1956, his speeches in parliamentary debate were extremely caustic, and no more so than when he proclaimed that the federal government, "by its actions in the Suez crisis, has made this month of November 1956, the most disgraceful period for Canada in the history of this nation."[258] He undoubtedly hurt Pearson, who was stung by his words but did quote them in his memoirs.

Another politician was also hurting, but in a different way, and had been for some time. Anthony Eden was a sick man. No matter how many operations he had endured in the past, no matter what medications he took now, the stress of his job, the criticism he endured, and the lack of rest he was getting all came together over Suez.

In early October, not long before the start of the war, his wife was hospitalized for a brief period. When he went to see her, he took ill while at the hospital, developed a temperature of 106° F, and was immediately admitted to the same institution himself. A couple of days later, after the fever subsided, he was released with the proviso that he slow down. He tried to do so, but failed. Later he wrote that the fever attacks — and there were many — "were in themselves so weakening that nobody could suffer from them and at the same time do a good day's work, let alone a night's work."[259] Yet Eden refused to slow down; he added, "a Prime Minister's job in this country, if it is conscientiously discharged, can begin at eight-thirty in the morning and may end at one or two the next morning."[260]

If he resigned, he was sure that his critics would simply say he had failed as a leader, had failed to win over the opposition, and had failed in his handling of the Suez situation. And because he believed that all of these conclusions were unfair, he felt he had to soldier on — and he did, but not for long.

On Tuesday, November 20, concerns about the Prime Minister's health were on the front pages of newspapers across the globe. A statement issued from 10 Downing Street the night before referred to "severe overstrain," and his personal physician, Sir Horace Evans, was said to be with him. Parliamentarians and the public were advised that all of Eden's appointments had been postponed or cancelled outright. They were also told that the Prime Minister had not taken any time off in over a year.

The news came as a severe shock to many in Britain and elsewhere. Eden had been seen in public recently, had attended official functions, and had been the principal spokesman and driving force behind Britain's decision to go to war. Without him, there probably would not have been a war. His supporters knew that; the public knew that; and in all likelihood, even Gamal Nasser knew that.

But now, with Eden sidelined and unable to function in his elected capacity, the nation waited and worried about what might happen. Richard Austen "Rab" Butler, Lord Privy Seal and Leader of the House of Commons, would be the temporary replacement and would preside over cabinet meetings until the Prime Minister was capable of carrying on. Initially, the official word was that the incapacity would be a brief one. Eden just needed some rest, both physically and emotionally. The former was known; the latter was becoming more and more evident with each day that passed. The Opposition in Parliament faulted him for almost everything he did. The public and press were divided or hostile, and increasingly members of Eden's own party were dissatisfied with his running of the country and his lack of success in Egypt. Many thought that Eden's program "failed to achieve what it was designed to achieve, and that the ceasefire agreement was the final, inconclusive half-measure of a series of miscalculations. He had taken only half the canal, and Nasser was still in power."[261] The critics added to the list of failings the blocked canal, the split with the U.S., and the dissention and divisiveness in the Commonwealth. There were other problems as well, such as Arab discontent and fuel shortages — so many that no one man could have dealt with them all.

Some party stalwarts stood up for Eden, and Rab Butler was among them. The Conservative Party Association had a scheduled gathering at Cambridge University, and the Lord Privy Seal was there to deliver the keynote address. Butler spoke in rather general terms about the state of the party, his own sense of where it was going, and his esteemed colleague and friend, Sir Anthony Eden. He told the members that, despite what they had read and heard concerning the Prime Minister, he was not ill. "He has simply had a hell of a time, and it is essential he should have a holiday for a few weeks." Butler concluded with a personal observation: "He has been submitted probably to more pressure and more attack than almost any statesman in our history."[262]

The upshot of the whole affair was that Sir Anthony and Lady Eden boarded a plane and flew to Jamaica for some rest, sun, and solitude at

Goldeneye, the island home of Ian Fleming, writer and creator of the suave, urbane James Bond. Fleming's wife, Ann, and Clarissa Eden were good friends, and the Flemings felt that the loan of their tropical cottage to the Prime Minister was the least they could do when he needed help. As he boarded the plane that would whisk him away from the rain and rancour of England, the obviously exhausted Eden told reporters: "I am assured that on my return to this country, I shall feel completely fit, ready to resume my duties at once and fully."[263]

That remained to be seen.

IN THE PERIOD WHEN the British were trying to absorb the fact that their prime minister and their country were both in difficulty, men in uniform were travelling from several points on the globe to the military staging point at Capodichino airfield near the city of Naples, Italy. Among them was the vanguard for many Canadians who would follow. The first four C-119 flying boxcars from 435 Squadron flew out of Edmonton to Downsview Airport in Toronto. There the planes were serviced and United Nations markings were painted on the fuselage, tail booms, and tops of the wings. In addition, several other planes from 436 Squadron transported equipment and supplies to Italy. Four C-119s crossed the Atlantic in each flight. Two North Star passenger planes carried necessary personnel who would handle administrative duties at the destination. At a later date, the *Magnificent* would bring heavier equipment and additional troops.

The days leading up to the arrival of the Canadians and other troops in Italy had been filled with high-level and generally frustrating talks by Hammarskjöld and Burns with President Nasser in Cairo. The Egyptian leader, whose troops had been soundly defeated in every Israeli and Allied exchange, remained as belligerent as ever, acting all the while as if his country had been the winner of the war. He was egged on by Soviets, who supplied both guns and backbone and did what they could to destroy everything Pearson and his colleagues at the UN had set in place.

Nasser said he did not want the Queen's Own Rifles in the policing force, and he got his wish. Then he said he might not accept peacekeepers from either Denmark or Norway, ostensibly because these countries were part of NATO. Then he said they would be acceptable after all — but then just as suddenly reversed himself and decided there should be no Scandinavian representation. Then he switched again. On the top of this intransigence, he decreed that he alone would decide where UN troops would go, how long they could stay, and, to a degree, what they could and could not do while they were in his country. He also wanted UNEF to clear the ships he had sunk in the canal. After all, its closure meant that no transit fees were being paid to his regime.

But Nasser still wanted General Burns to command the peacekeeping force. He liked, trusted, and respected this military man who he knew would stand up to the Israelis.

Pearson was well aware of Nasser's desire to keep Burns at the helm of UNEF, and to that end he got a blunt, if not particularly diplomatic, message through to Cairo. In effect, our Minister of External Affairs told Nasser that if Canadians could not be part of UNEF, the Egyptian could go to hell. Since Nasser wanted Burns, he had to take other Canadians. The upshot was that Nasser backed down, and administrative troops came from Canada.

As Pearson expected, his old nemesis, the *Globe and Mail*, ridiculed this arrangement, both in the reporting of the decision and in editorials about the move. On November 20, for example, the paper faulted Hammarskjöld for bowing to Nasser's demands that "such units Canada sends to the Middle East must be administrative in nature." Then, with caustic arrogance, the paper editorially dismissed such troops, calling them "a typewriter army."[264] In researching this book, I talked to former Canadian peacekeepers who are still angry at the reference. They resent the fact that, in the *Globe*'s view, friends who died trying to keep the peace were only a part of this typewriter army. I rarely mentioned to these veterans who served so well that on November 21, the paper said they were really just part of an "international farce."[265]

One of the ongoing problems in the early hours and days after the ceasefire in Port Said was that without the Anglo-French troops, the town became a kind of no man's land where armed Egyptians roamed free. There was looting, sniper firing, and understandable reluctance by the occupied to cede control to the foreigners and their guns. For this reason, neither the English nor the French wanted to pull back, at least before the UN peacekeepers were on scene. This state of affairs, like the composition of the peacekeeping force, was the subject of hours and hours of negotiation in Cairo, London, New York, and Paris. Finally, the Allies announced their projected departure dates, and then peacekeepers were on the ground in Port Said.

The first to arrive were Norwegian soldiers, who flew into the former Royal Air Force base at Abu Seweir, a few miles west of Ismailia, and then went by train from there to Port Said itself. They arrived at noon on November 21 and were met by a spirited and generally welcoming crowd. According to one paper, some "20,000 wildly shouting Egyptians engulfed the 190 blue-helmeted Norwegian infantrymen at the railroad station and clung to them for the 45 minutes it took them to march to their camp site." The same reporter who watched the arrival added, "It was the first explosion of popular feeling since the British and French forces seized Port Said and Port Fuad." The newsman reported that the greeting "appeared to be made up of one-third wild enthusiasm for the UN troops, one-third cheers for Egyptian President Nasser and one-third hostility to the British and French forces."[266] In part, the response was a reflection of Radio Cairo broadcasts that urged the citizens of Port Said to welcome the UN contingent.

The first group of twenty Canadians landed at Abu Suweir on November 24. Their flight, operated by Swissair, left Capodichino at 6:24 that morning, and it would be one of the last with the Swiss company. A short time later, its contract to ferry the soldiers expired, and after that Royal Canadian Air Force planes did the shuttle on a regular basis.

The Canadians in the contingent descended from their plane into scorching desert heat. All were wearing battledress, with full kit and side arms. Once on the ground, the nine officers and eleven men were welcomed to Egypt by Brigadier-General Amin Hermy, an Egyptian Army liaison officer seconded to the UN. As soon as possible after a brief inspection on the Tarmac, they headed for their quarters and got rid of their heavy jackets. Then their acclimatization to their new surroundings began.

The quarters where the men would live had been built by the British several years earlier but had also been bombed by them in the hours that preceded the Port Said landings. There was some structural damage, but not a lot, because the bombs had been intended for Egyptian aircraft parked near the base airstrip. The quarters, however, were Spartan: long, single-storey limestone buildings roofed in corrugated iron; they never cooled much, even at night. Nevertheless, they provided some respite from the heat and blowing sand.

Initially, the Canadians were involved in mine identification near El Cap, a short train ride north. The job was dangerous, painstaking, and necessary. Each minefield located was marked with tape for safety reasons, and each mine was marked for subsequent removal. Joining the men on the job was an army medic; fortunately, the morphine he carried did not have to be used. The operation concluded safely, and then some of the soldiers involved went swimming in the Suez Canal in an attempt to cool down.

The men complained about the conditions under which they had to live, and, to a certain extent, they had reason to do so. They "were not permitted off the camp except in connection with their United Nations work" and, as a result, referred to the place "as a concentration camp and to themselves as prisoners-of-war of the Egyptians."[267]

Though these first Canadians had few complaints about the Egyptians they encountered, the location of the quarters caused much grumbling. According to a reporter who wrote about it for readers back home, the setting was less than inviting. He pointed out that "Canadian troops have been stationed in some dismal places and Abu Suweir must rank as one of the most dismal of all."[268] Understandably, it was never mentioned on recruiting posters in Ottawa, Red Deer, or Moncton.

But finally, Canadians were on the ground, learning on the job, adapting to circumstance, and keeping the peace at a forlorn outpost in a foreign land. They eventually would become very good at it.

CHAPTER TWENTY-ONE

The Fall of Anthony Eden

ON DECEMBER 29, 1956, the Royal Canadian Navy aircraft carrier *Magnificent* inched back from the pier in Halifax, then turned and slowly eased out of the harbour past Georges Island and Point Pleasant Park towards a grey and heaving sea. Finally, after Nasser's foot-dragging and megalomaniacal stubbornness, the last of Canada's Suez force was en route to the Middle East. On board that day were some "400 officers and men, 230 vehicles and four Otter aircraft."[269] Many, perhaps most, of the soldiers on board knew little of ships. This trip, they would remember.

The embarkation had been a quiet one — literally. Because the Navy did not want all these soldiers tramping around the decks in army boots, each man who boarded was given white sneakers to wear while he was on the ship. This certainly cut down on the noise, and it made exercising on the decks possible. Daily calisthenics were mandatory during the trip.

Halifax weather during the departure was rather benign. Some wet snow fell, but there was little wind, and the temperature was 35° Fahrenheit. These conditions were soon to change, however. Within hours, the air was colder, heavy snow began to fall, and fierce winds swept much of eastern North America. From Boston to Maine to Newfoundland, the first major storm of the season closed highways, tore down power lines, and stranded travellers whose cars were stuck in waist-deep drifts. A foot of snow immobilized New England. A ferry, a dragger, and a twin-masted schooner were all driven aground in the harbour the *Magnificent* had just vacated.

But the ship made good time, if in a rather circuitous way.

Captain A.B. Fraser-Harris was a seasoned master, and rather than risk his ship, her cargo, and all the first-time mariners to the worst of the gale, he took his ship farther south than would normally have been the case. Still, the house-high swells of the North Atlantic were not well-loved by the boys from the Prairies, from Ontario, or from tiny towns that were far from the sea. But the ship sailed on; the sailors on board showed the newcomers around and taught them naval terminology. When the *Magnificent* passed Gibraltar and moved into the Mediterranean, the soldiers saw the Rock for the first time.

Farther east, in Port Said, the Allied withdrawal continued. In the streets, UNEF soldiers patrolled with Egyptian police, and together they coped as best they could with occasional disturbances. In the harbour, two thousand Anglo-French soldiers crammed into *Dilwara*, the troop-ship that would take them home from the war. As well, "an armada of ships of all kinds steamed towards Port Said to take on others, and the UN police force ... grew as the British and French sped their departure."[270] The commanding officer of the force addressed his men, thanked them for their role in the endeavour, and told them they had nothing to apologize for. They had done their job and they had done it well. General Stockwell, however, declined to announce a specific date when all his troops would be out. Doing so, he feared, might only increase the propensity of trou-blemakers to make the final departure as unpleasant as possible.

While all this was happening, negotiations were being held elsewhere concerning the Israeli pullback. These talks were not going well. David Ben Gurion flatly refused to give up the territory his troops had overrun in their advance against the Egyptians. The more Burns, Hammarskjöld, or even Eisenhower pushed, the firmer the Israeli resolve. While the Anglo-French gains were relinquished, albeit with recriminations direct-ed mainly against the Americans and their lack of support for the war, the Israelis decided that the territory they had captured, they would keep.

Because Ben Gurion regarded the land his troops now controlled "as a buffer shielding his nation from Arab attacks ... he resisted mightily international efforts to expel Israeli forces from Sinai."[271] Finally, it was the newly re-elected American president who made some gains with Ben Gurion. Eisenhower wrote to the Israeli prime minister, reminding him of all the support the United States had given his country and saying he hoped that the positive relationship between their nations could continue. Eisenhower chastened Ben Gurion for not pulling back in Sinai and indicated that if he continued to be so obstreperous, he could not automatically expect help from the U.S. Then, at a time when Russia was still indicating the desire for more influence in the Middle East, the American president played his trump card. "He told Israel it could expect no U.S. help if Israel's delay resulted in Russian attack."[272]

From that time on, Ben Gurion became more reasonable, but the relinquishment of the conquered land was a slow and painstaking process. UNEF peacekeepers, including Canadian combat engineers, began to clear Israeli land mines in the western part of Sinai, not too far from the Suez Canal. The job was dangerous and time-consuming, made all the more so "by significant Israeli denial measures: the roads had been dug up with bulldozers, the rail lines torn up every 50 metres, and there were uncharted minefields everywhere."[273]

General Burns met with Moshe Dayan to discuss the situation, and while the Israeli general indicated his troops were now about thirty miles east of the canal, they were not about to pull back any more than that. The meeting had lasted an hour, and as a result, Dayan admitted that any future Israeli withdrawal would involve political matters that he was not empowered to consider. At the end of the discussion, Burns showed obvious irritation with the lack of clear-cut answers, but he nonetheless continued to fulfill the United Nations mandate that he had been given. We have no way of knowing whether he felt the $18,000 to $25,000 per year that he was being paid was worth the frustration.

There was more communication between Eisenhower and Ben Gurion with regard to the pullback, and it was obvious the Jewish Head of State found the withdrawal painful. After all, for several weeks, he had marvelled at the Israeli success in the war. On November 7, for example, he had told the Knesset that the Israeli success in Sinai "was the greatest and most splendid military operation in the chronicles of our people, and one of the greatest in the history of the nations."[274]

Two months to the day later, Golda Meier, then the Israeli foreign minister, met with representatives of the countries involved in UNEF in order to explain the Jewish position to them. She reiterated the fears her country had in pulling back, because as yet no one knew what would happen after such a withdrawal. "Israel did not know how long UNEF would remain in the area or whether Egyptians would return with military forces to re-establish the bases for fedayeen raids on Israeli territory."[275] Meier told her audience that it was this uncertainty that was the real concern in her country.

Eventually, however, following hundreds of hours of discussion at the highest levels at the UN and in the capitals of the countries involved with the fallout from the Suez war, Israel did pull back, not only from the Sinai peninsula but ultimately from the Gaza Strip as well. Coupled with the latter move was the UN reassurance that a UNEF contingent would be placed at Sharm el-Sheikh so that the Gulf of Aqaba would remain open for Israeli shipping. At the same time, United Nations peacekeeping troops moved into the Gaza Strip and policed it for several years.

ANTHONY EDEN HAD DECAMPED for Jamaica at a time when the Suez situation was far from resolved. But even though he was removed from daily debate in the House of Commons and the pressure that being there entailed, he was not exactly out of mind. Britain did agree to remove troops from Egypt while the Prime Minister was away, and because that decision was of such importance, there was criticism both within his party and outside it that Eden was away when he was needed most. But Eden did communicate with his staff and one or two Cabinet members. "I arranged to keep in touch with urgent decisions by cable," Eden recalled. "While I was away, the Lord Privy Seal, Mr. Butler, presided at Cabinet meetings. He and his colleagues kept me informed and we exchanged opinions on the decisions they took."[276]

Eden's messages arrived in the U.K. at a time when the failure to achieve the ends desired in Egypt was resonating in various quarters. In the public mind, the outcome was depressing. The press was critical, and in the ruling party, the bickering over who was to blame was more noticeable. All three of these groups needed a scapegoat.

In mid-December, Canadian High Commissioner Norman Robertson sent a long, detailed, secret telegram to Lester Pearson, in which he commented on the mood in Britain as he saw it: "Now that it is becoming increasingly difficult to hide the fact that the Anglo-French intervention has been a failure, the tendency to make America the public scapegoat has assumed disturbing proportion."[277] Robertson's worries were well founded. He also viewed with alarm how politically useful this anti-U.S. factor was in both France and Britain. While from his point of view, the attitude was more pronounced in France, it was being promulgated in Britain by a source that he felt was alarming. "We have reason to believe," he wrote, "that Sir Anthony Eden last week sent messages from Jamaica encouraging more 'standing up to the Americans' in ministerial statements."[278] Of course, Eden makes no mention of any such thing in his memoirs.

But Eden had other problems, some of which were more widespread than he may have realized. Even before he left for his rest in the tropics, there had been an element of discontent among his colleagues about his inadequacies in governance. Now that he was out of the country, the proponents of change became bolder and more outspoken, and the move to dump Eden increased. The press picked up on this and speculated on it. In a Reuters dispatch from London, two weeks after Eden left, his fall was predicted: "Prime Minister Eden's absence during Suez crisis developments brought speculation … about a change in leadership. As the crisis moves from one vital phase to another, some Conservatives [Eden's party] openly predict a change of leadership soon."[279] The crisis in Britain's economy, which had been largely brought about by the adventure in Egypt, was also hurting Eden's cause.

In mid-December, Pearson flew to London for talks with senior officials in the British government. On his return to Ottawa, he sent a memorandum to St. Laurent that detailed some of the impressions he got from the time overseas.

"There is no doubt in my mind now that the whole ill-conceived and ill-judged enterprise, at least on the British side, was Eden's," wrote Pearson. "Eden was the active, determined and confident leader of the enterprise, showing qualities of vigour and resolution worthy of a better cause."[280] Pearson added that after his discussions with Selwyn Lloyd, Rab Butler, and Harold Macmillan, he felt that Eden's days as prime minister were numbered. And he was right.

Eden returned from Jamaica and was back in Parliament on December 17. The welcome for him was rather subdued. The Opposition members were largely silent, while his own supporters were respectful but not particularly effusive in their reaction to his presence. Judging from press accounts and materials that are on the public record about Eden at this time, the overwhelming feeling seems to have been that this prime minister would not be long in office.

And he was not.

Over Christmas that year and then in early January, Eden had a recurrence of the fever that had plagued him for so long. He tried to cope as best he could, but to no avail. Three medical specialists who examined him gave the same advice. The Prime Minister was a sick man, and in order to retain some semblance of health, he would have to step down now. At 5:00 p.m. on January 9, 1957, he held his last Cabinet meeting, "a sad and moving occasion,"[281] according to Selwyn Lloyd. That evening, Eden went to Buckingham Palace and handed his resignation to Her Majesty, the Queen.

Harold Macmillan accepted the reins of power.

THE SUEZ CRISIS WAS ESSENTIALLY OVER before Eden's resignation was tendered. In the weeks leading up to it, more and more peacekeepers had poured into Egypt, and detailed and drawn-out negotiations continued concerning which troops would go where and when. Throughout this period, General Burns worked with little rest to bring about success in the mandate that he had been given. That was why he went to Port Said in person on December 22 to watch for himself the final departure of the Anglo-French troops from Egyptian soil. There were the expected final military parades, the lowering of the flags of Britain and France, and the raising of the blue and white UN banner in their stead. As the last of the departing troops boarded ships that would take them away, fighter jets screamed low across the waterfront "to remind the Egyptians that the Allied air power was still ready to counter any resumption of hostilities."[282] There was none.

The next day, thousands of rapturous Egyptians poured into the streets of Port Said, dynamited the statue of Ferdinand de Lesseps at the mouth of the canal, and declared themselves free from the Anglo-French presence they had resented for generations.

For the next several years, the peacekeepers of the United Nations would remain a presence in this ancient land. Their role was necessary, praiseworthy, and at times tragic.

CHAPTER TWENTY-TWO

Peacekeeping in Egypt

THOUGH THE HISTORY of Canadian and United Nations peacekeeping in Egypt has been told elsewhere and is not technically part of the Suez Crisis as such, a brief account of the endeavour is worthwhile here. In the previous chapters, the reasons Canadians went to Egypt have been discussed. This chapter will touch on the deployment, the function, and the kind of contributions Canadians made in this historic and volatile area of the world.

The rustic conditions under which our troops lived when they first came to Abu Suweir were not particularly good for morale. From the time of their arrival there on November 24, they had done as much as they could to spruce up the place and make it more or less habitable. By mid-December, there were 295 Canadian soldiers in Egypt, the bulk of whom were operating out of the one base. Living conditions had improved, but the Canadians still chafed at many of the issues with which they had to contend. Because Egyptians guarded the compound, no one could leave unless it was for UN work, and then they had to have a pass to get out. This state of affairs was annoying until it was eased.

But the main irritants included being crammed, several men together, in small quarters with little to do, having to cope with a 10:00 p.m. to 6:00 a.m. curfew, and existing without reading material of almost any kind. "One hut with 12 men in it had one magazine. Each soldier passed it on to his neighbour after reading one article and waited for it to come around again,"[283] one newspaper reporter wrote, describing the situation. Initially, there was no sports equipment at all, so most of the men passed the time trying to fix up the buildings, raking the sand around them, and, insofar as they could, cleaning their quarters. But even the cleanup was not easy because virtually all the supplies needed were on the *Magnificent*, and she had not yet arrived. For Christmas that year, some of the troops decided that they were going to have their own Christmas trees, no matter what, but these were in short supply in the desert. A few two-by-fours nailed together with makeshift tinsel served the purpose.

The holiday season was a rather bittersweet time. The camaraderie was good, but the loneliness for some of the younger soldiers was palpable. The officers, while missing home themselves, did what they could to ensure that being in Egypt was as pleasant as possible for their men. Back at home, the post office announced that there was more Christmas mail for military personnel overseas than at any time since the mid-war years. More than seventy thousand pounds of letters and assorted gifts went to those serving in Europe, while two plane loads were transported to the Middle East peacekeepers. For them, mail call was the highlight of the season.

But for those young men who had signed up for the adventure of a lifetime by going to Egypt, the idea had already lost some of its original appeal. Most expected, of course, that they would have to spend only one Christmas where they were. Already troop rotation was being discussed, not only by those in Abu Suweir, but by senior commanders in Ottawa.

Finally, on January 10, the carrier got to Port Said with all the equipment that was so urgently required by the men in Egypt. On the ship that day was the largest group of Canadian soldiers in the first contingent to serve with UNEF. Their presence was both welcome and needed, and their performance would be chronicled for the folks back home by newspaper reporters who came on the ship as well.

But at least one correspondent never actually got to complete his trip. A *Toronto Telegram* writer tried to go with the soldiers, but he ran afoul of someone in the ship's company. The media man decided to stow away, and while his plans might have been reasonably creative, they were unsuccessful. John Maclean had a reputation for crazy antics, and the one he attempted to pull on the *Magnificent* ranked right up there with his best. He had been sent to cover the departure of the ship from Halifax, but then, on the spur of the moment, decided to go along for the ride. He "had gotten drunk and hidden somewhere below deck, with a case of cheese sandwiches and a suitcase full of Scotch. He was discovered soon after the *Maggie* had gotten underway, and was put ashore with the pilot."[284] No one knows what happened to the Scotch or the sandwiches.

Most of the young soldiers had never been out of Canada, so the medics among them cautioned everyone about drinking the local water. Some heeded the advice "and instead put their faith in whiskey."[285] There were also those who disregarded health warnings of a different kind. "Lectures and notices warning that syphilis could be contacted from local prostitutes or hepatitis from a nearby tattoo artist only seemed to increase their business."[286] This was in spite of the strict rules about needing a UN pass to get off the compound property.

While Canadian soldiers who came on the *Magnificent* were getting accustomed to their new surroundings, high-level talks were being held at the United Nations in New York concerning the removal of the ships blocking the Suez Canal. Britain and France offered to do the job; because they had the necessary equipment, they could do it far faster than anyone else. Initially, this idea was turned down by Nasser, because once the Allies were out of his country, he wanted them to stay out. In time, the British and French did do salvage work, but to appease Nasser, "their naval crews would be dressed as civilians and would be protected by small detachments [of guards]"[287]; the guards were primarily troops from Finland and Sweden. Subsequently, salvage vessels from other countries, including Germany, helped. "The Canal was at length cleared and Hammarskjöld himself watched the last block ship lifted on the 25th of March."[288] The canal was open, and would be for the next ten years. Sadly, another war would break out then between Israel and Egypt, and the waterway would be closed once more — this time for eight years.

THE UNLOADING OF THE *MAGNIFICENT* AT PORT SAID was done in six days, the shortest time ever. The peacekeepers disembarked as soon as they were allowed on shore, and for those who had not enjoyed their first ocean crossing, setting foot on dry land was greatly appreciated. The trip had been a new experience, but for many, being seasick was not a pleasant part of the adventure. The supplies for the peacekeepers were off-loaded to the pier, then hefted onto trucks and taken to Abu Suweir and elsewhere. Some items remained in Port Said, where they were secured and later removed to other locations as needed. The soldiers also exchanged their shipboard sneakers for army boots.

The last items of cargo to leave the carrier were the four Otter aircraft. They had been taken apart prior to the Halifax departure and partially crated during the trip in order to allow for the best possible use of space on the ship. As soon as mechanics finished putting each machine back together, it was pushed to one end of the carrier deck, fired up, and flown away. Members of the ship's company watched each departure and marvelled at the skill of the flying officers as each plane roared down the deck and lifted into the sky. When the second single-engined Otter departed, an unexpected crosswind came close to sweeping the little plane over the side of the ship. Fortunately, George Foster, the pilot at the controls, reacted quickly and got the aircraft in the air without incident. All four Otters were flown to Gamil airport, and each pilot was subsequently airlifted back in the helicopter that was part of the equipment normally carried on the carrier. Soon afterwards, the *Magnificent* departed Port Said. The troop transport was its last major trip, as the vessel would be decommissioned shortly afterwards.

Now that the personnel and supplies for the Canadian part of the peacekeeping mission were in Egypt, they were integrated into UNEF and stationed in places where General Burns and his staff judged they would be most useful. These allocations took some time, and further talks were needed with Egypt and Israel before they were completely implemented. Prisoner of war exchanges took place as negotiated as well.

Gradually, the Israelis pulled back in Sinai; as they did so, UNEF troops moved farther east, ultimately reaching the long, sandy wasteland border area that separates Israel from Egypt between the Mediterranean and the Gulf of Aqaba. As the UN forces advanced, the Egyptian Frontier Police followed, and it was this group who was entrusted with maintaining civil control. The first major town General Burns and his forces brought under UN command was Al Arish, on the northern coast of the Sinai Peninsula. For a time, the United Nations established a headquarters here, but the long-term intent was to bring UNEF to the Gaza Strip, still under Israeli control, and to Sharm el Sheikh.

On the afternoon of March 4, General Burns received word that these two moves were in the offing. In a message that day, Israeli General Moshe Dayan signalled that "he had been ordered by his Government to get his troops out of the Gaza Strip and Sharm el Sheikh as quickly as possible."[289] Peacekeepers moved into both, and by the end of March 1957, UNEF was firmly established in what would become a ten-year routine. In rather general terms, "UNEF was situated on a linear buffer zone observing movements and investigating incidents."[290]

OVER THE YEARS, hundreds of young Canadians served on the UNEF peacekeeping mission in Egypt. Each soldier came home with his own recollection of the time: often boring, sometimes exciting, and occasionally dangerous. The best times for most were the breaks in the routine, no matter what they were. Entertainers from Canada and elsewhere showed up from time to time, performed for the troops, ate with them, posed for pictures, signed autographs, and left.

The chance to swim in the Mediterranean was welcome and safe, compared to the same thing in the Red Sea. There, Canadian signallers heard the stories and sometimes watched the antics of Finnish soldiers whose idea of fun was swimming in a shark-infested area. "For excitement one Finnish soldier would attract a shark in the Red Sea and then swim for shore. His comrades on the cliffs, with rifles and automatic weapons, would shoot at the shark for target practice," wrote historian Fred Gaffen. He added the wry comment: "While the Finns suffered no casualties the same cannot be said for the sharks."[291]

In contrast to the deprivation at Abu Suweir in the early days of UNEF, the facilities and comforts available to the troops gradually improved as the years passed. There were more sports venues: rudimentary desert golf, shinny on almost any kind of wood or cement surface, softball, and basketball on makeshift courts. Soldiers wrote home, played cards, availed themselves of alcohol that was readily available, kept diaries, and took part in civic-minded endeavours that often involved fundraising for local humanitarian causes.

Canadian soldiers patrolled what was called the Armistice Demarcation Line (ADL) between Israel and Egypt. These patrols were, according to the UN mandate, only on Egyptian land. Generally, the purpose was to prevent everything from theft to sabotage, from fedayeen attacks to people taking potshots at individuals or groups who happened to be visible just across the ADL. Movement was prohibited in a five-hundred-metre-deep zone, and the UN took into custody anyone it caught in this zone.[292]

Trooper Bill Lemaire, of the 8th Canadian Hussars, was often involved in these patrols during his Egyptian tour. "We would pick a guy up," Lemaire explained, "take any weapon he might have had, and then turn him over to the Egyptian police. We rarely heard what they did with these guys though. They probably kept the gun and let him go."[293]

Lemaire and those with him, and others in the years before and after, carried out these patrols in roughly the same manner all the time. "We always went in pairs," he told the author, "and often with a German shepherd police dog in the vehicle with us. We were not allowed to travel at night — ever."

The white Jeeps used for the job were clearly painted with the UN insignia. The route followed was essentially a long rectangle — thirty-five miles along the border, across the clearly marked five-hundred-metre zone, and then back in the opposite direction on the inner side of the rectangle. Within the enclosed area was a minefield, and there lay a constant danger that became apparent with tragic results on November 27, 1964.

That day, two UN Jeeps were travelling along the ADL when in the leading vehicle Trooper Adrian Bons and Corporal Paul Wallace, both of the 8th Hussars, noticed a male figure crouched and watching them from some scrub brush in the restricted area. Wallace yelled at the man to approach. When there was no response, he yelled again, as the sable-coloured German shepherd in the Jeep glared and growled. When the man started to run, Bons gunned the motor, and in no time the shepherd had cornered the stranger. By this time, he seemed more terrified of Tiger, the dog, than of either peacekeeper. The man was loaded into the Jeep, and as it turned around, one wheel ran onto a land mine that none of them saw. The three men and Tiger all died in the explosion that resulted, while the two Canadians in the second Jeep watched with abject horror. Today, the graves of Paul Wallace and Adrian Bons are located in the Gaza War Cemetery. The two had gone to a faraway country to keep the peace and died doing it.

From time to time, Canadian peacekeepers in Egypt encountered weather that they had never experienced before. Trooper Lemaire mentions a sandstorm that was more ferocious than any January blizzard he remembered back home. "We were more or less marooned in a tent," he explained, "and you couldn't see, you couldn't breathe, and you couldn't go anywhere — even if you had to. The next day they had to use a bulldozer to get us out and clear the road."

For most peacekeepers, the tour of duty in Egypt lasted twelve months, and training was done in Canada before departure. The training included, among many other things, driving on sand and identifying land mines. There was, of course, no preparation possible for a matter that involved most of the young Canadians at some time or other. Homesickness was always a problem, but the soldiers kept busy and coped.

As the routine of living, patrolling, policing, and learning the ways of a foreign country became more familiar, the soldiers from Canada also got the chance to see some of the world beyond their compound. Those who wanted went on leave to Alexandria, Cairo, Beirut, and elsewhere. But "home," in the latter stages of UNEF, was a camp about a mile from the town of Rafah, on the southwest border of the Gaza Strip. In addition to the main camp, two satellite compounds were located on the international border to the south. The soldiers rotated through the three, spending six weeks in each.

Finally, the policing in the desert did come to an end — and in a way that was both expected and abrupt. Again, storm clouds were rising in the Middle East, but this time, at least, Britain and France were not involved. Instead, the age-old animosities among the nations of the area led to what history has called the Six Day War. In the face of the turmoil about to erupt, Gamal Nasser exercised the authority he had demanded of the UN ten and a half years earlier. He ordered UNEF troops out of his country. This expulsion involved Canadians, who departed with their heads held high.

AFTERWORD

MUCH HAS BEEN WRITTEN about Lester Pearson's proposal for a United Nations police force in the Middle East. In most accounts, the creation, function, and performance of UNEF was called a success. There were pitfalls and problems, of course, but the overall result of the endeavour was both reassuring and surprising — reassuring because the threat to world peace that existed when it was formed was ameliorated, and surprising because it is doubtful that those who set up UNEF in the fall of 1956 would have envisioned its existence a decade hence.

For Lester Pearson, it meant not only the Nobel Prize but also a lock on leadership of the Liberals that ultimately led to 24 Sussex Drive. As prime minister of Canada, Pearson led a country he loved — a country that never returned the affection with a parliamentary majority. Nevertheless, UNEF is one of the triumphs of his time.

The creation of the peacekeeping body had other ramifications. In fact, "the UNEF experience also set the tone and form for future UN Peacekeeping operations."[294] And Canadians have been part of many of these, more of them than any other nation. We have become good at peacekeeping, and we have achieved varying degrees of success each time the UN has asked for our help. One historian, referring to UNEF and the Canadians, claimed that "they left behind a record so credible that they were asked to contribute again in 1973."[295]

United Nations Emergency Force Middle East, or UNEFME, existed from 1973 to 1979. Also known as UNEF II, this mission was intended to lend support for another Egyptian-Israeli ceasefire that followed the Yom

Kippur War. Canadians were again involved, much as before, and often in the same places they were during UNEF. One highly respected veteran of the mission, Air Force Captain H.C. Fielding, recalled several of the same kinds of problems that were prevalent in the earlier tenure. He talked of storms so severe that sand had to be shovelled out of tents where Canadians lived, of deaths of nine peacekeepers in a single day (in this case in a Buffalo aircraft that was shot down over Damascus), and of the security prevalent in the air and on the ground at the time.[296]

But UNEF set the standard. In fact, Brian Urquhart, former Under Secretary-General of the United Nations, called UNEF "a turning point for the United Nations ... a new kind of military operation that could actually achieve important results." He also added that in his opinion, "UNEF was a great victory of common sense, innovation, hard work, and intelligent leadership."[297] Added to that was the opinion of Briton Michael Harbottle, a former Chief of Staff for the UN peacekeeping force in Cyprus, who has written that "the performance of UNEF and its achievements in its peacekeeping role are not subject to argument. Placed in its proper perspective it is a story of success."[298] And even though there were many who laboured with him, it was Pearson who saw to it that UNEF became a reality. With his dogged determination, tenacity, charm, and vision, he pushed the United Nations into making a better world. As Michael Kovrig, Media and Communications Officer for the Permanent Mission of Canada to the United Nations, expressed it recently, "Lester Pearson was well regarded in peacekeeping circles."[299] And he was rewarded by a grateful world with the Nobel Prize for Peace. The man had truly earned the accolade.

BIBLIOGRAPHY

Aburish, Said K. *Nasser: The Last Arab*. New York: Thomas Dunne Books, 2004.

Barker, A.J. *Suez: the Seven Day War*. London: Faber and Faber, 1964.

Bar-On, Mordechai. *The Gates of Gaza*. New York: St. Martin's Griffin, 1994.

Bar-Zohar, Michael. *Ben-Gurion: A Biography*. New York: Delacorte, 1977.

Beaufre, Andre. *The Suez Expedition 1956*. Translated by Richard Barry. London: Faber and Faber, 1969.

Bothwell, Robert, Ian Drummond, and John English. *Canada Since 1945: Power, Politics, and Provincialism*. Toronto: University of Toronto Press, 1981.

Bothwell, Robert. *Pearson: His Life and World*, Toronto: McGraw-Hill Ryerson, 1978.

Brown, Craig, ed. *The Illustrated History of Canada*, Toronto: Key Porter, 1997.

Burns, Lt.-Gen. E.L.M. *Between Arab and Israeli*. Toronto: Clarke, Irwin & Company, 1962.

Catterall, Peter, ed. *The Macmillan Diaries: The Cabinet Years 1950-1957*. London: Pan Books, 2003.

Dayan, Major-General Moshe. *Diary of the Sinai Campaign*. New York: Schocken, 1967.

Donaghy, Greg, ed. *Documents on Canadian External Relations, Volume 22*. Ottawa: Department of Foreign Affairs and International Trade, 2001.

Dupuy, Colonel Trevor N. *Elusive Victory*. New York: Harper & Row, 1978.

Eden, Sir Anthony. *Full Circle*, London: Cassell, 1960.

English, John. *The Worldly Years: The Life of Lester Pearson, Volume II: 1949-1972*. Toronto: Alfred A. Knopf Canada, 1992.

Eveland, Wilbur Crane. *Ropes of Sand*, New York: W.W. Norton & Company, 1980.

Feldman, Burton. *The Nobel Prize*. New York: Arcade Publishing, 2000.

Fullick, Roy and Geoffrey Powell. *Suez: The Double War*. London: Hamish Hamilton, 1979.

Gaffen, Fred. *In the Eye of the Storm*. Ottawa: Deneau & Wayne, 1987.

Gardam, Colonel John. *The Canadian Peacekeeper*, Burnstown: General Store, 1992.

Granatstein, J.L. and David Bercuson. *War and Peacekeeping*. Toronto: Key Porter Books, 1991.

Granatstein, J.L. and Norman Hillmer. *Battle Lines: Eyewitness Accounts from Canada's Military History*. Toronto: Thomas Allen Publishers, 2004.

Greenhous, Brereton. *Dragoon: The Centennial History of the Royal Canadian Dragoons, 1883-1983*. Belleville: Guild of the Royal Canadian Dragoons, 1983.

Harbottle, Michael. *The Blue Berets*, London: Leo Cooper, 1971.

Heikal, Mohamed H. *Cutting the Lion's Tale*. New York: Arbor House, 1987.

Henriques, Robert. *A Hundred Hours to Suez*, New York: The Viking Press, 1957.

Humphreys, Andrew and Siona Jenkins. *Egypt*. Victoria: Lonely Planet Publications, 2002.

Karabell, Zachary. *Parting the Desert: The Creation of the Suez Canal*. New York: Alfred A. Knopf, 2003.

Katz, Samuel M. *Soldier Spies: Israeli Military Intelligence*, Novato, CA: Presidio, 1992.

Kyle, Keith. *Suez*, New York: St. Martin's Press, 1991.

Lloyd, Selwyn. *Suez 1956: A Personal Account*, New York: Mayflower Books, 1978.

Love, Kennett. *Suez: The Twice-Fought War*, New York: McGraw-Hill, 1969.

Macmillan, Harold. *Riding the Storm: 1956-1959*. London: Macmillan, 1971.

Maloney, Sean. *Canada and UN Peacekeeping*. St. Catherines: Vanwell Publishing Limited, 2002.

Mansfield, Peter. *The British in Egypt*. New York: Hold, Rinehart and Winston, 1971.

Martin, Lawrence. *The Presidents and the Prime Ministers*. Toronto: Doubleday Canada, 1982.

McCreery, Christopher. *The Canadian Honours System*. Toronto: Dundurn Press, 2005.

Morton, Desmond. *A Military History of Canada*. Edmonton: Hurtig Publishers, 1985.

Mosley, Leonard. *Dulles: A Biography of Eleanor, Allen, and John Foster Dulles and Their Family Network*, New York: The Dial Press, 1978.

Nash, Knowlton. *History on the Run*. Toronto: McClelland and Stewart, 1984.

Nasser, Gamal. *The Philosophy of the Revolution*, Washington: Public Affairs Press, 1955.

Neff, Donald. *Warriors at Suez*. New York: The Linden Press, 1981.

Nutting, Anthony. *No End of a Lesson*. London: Constable, 1967.

Pearson, Geoffrey A.H. *Seize the Day*. Ottawa: Carleton University Press, 1993.

Pearson, Lester B. *Mike, Volume 2*. Toronto: University of Toronto Press, 1973.

Robertson, Terence. *Crisis: The Inside Story of the Suez Conspiracy*. Toronto: McClelland and Stewart, 1964.

Stursberg, Peter. *Lester Pearson and the American Dilemma*, Toronto: Doubleday Canada, 1980.

Stursberg, Peter. *Lester Pearson and the Dream of Unity*, Toronto: Doubleday Canada, 1978.

Thomas, Hugh. *The Suez Affair*. London: Weidenfeld and Nicolson, 1966.

Thordarson, Bruce. *Lester Pearson: Diplomat and Politician*. Toronto: Oxford University Press, 1974.

Thorpe, D.R. *Eden*, London: Pimlico, 2004.

Urquhart, Brian. *A Life in Peace and War*, New York: Harper & Row, 1987.

Varble, Derek. *Essential Histories: The Suez Crisis 1956*. Oxford: Osprey Publishing, 2003.

Verbeek, Bertjan. *Decision-making in Great Britain During the Suez Crisis*. Aldershot: Ashgate, 2003.

Worthington, Larry. *The Spur and the Sprocket*. Gagetown: The Royal Canadian Dragoons, 1968

Worthington, Peter. *Looking for Trouble*. Toronto: Key Porter, 1984.

NOTES

1   Geoffrey A.H. Pearson, author interview, July 25, 2005.
2   Mary MacDonald, quoted in Peter Stursberg, *Lester Pearson and the Dream of Unity* (Toronto: Doubleday Canada, 1978), 45.
3   Patricia Hannah, author interview, August 8, 2005.
4   Lester Pearson, *Mike*, Vol. 2 (Toronto: University of Toronto Press, 1973), 275.
5   Lester Pearson, *Mike*, 275–276.
6   Burton Feldman, *The Nobel Prize* (New York: Arcade Publishing, 2000), 42.
7   Feldman, *Nobel Prize*, 25.
8   Feldman, *Nobel Prize*, 41.
9   Helge Kjollesdal, Director of Information, University of Oslo, e-mail to the author, March 10, 2005.
10 Bruce Macdonald, "Pearson Saved World From War Over Suez Nobel Chairman Says," *Toronto Star* (December 10, 1957), 2.
11 Zachary Karabell, *Parting the Desert: The Creation of the Suez Canal* (New York: Alfred A. Knopf, 2003), 76.
12 Ibid.
13 Sir Denis Brogan, *The Development of Modern France 1870-1939* (London: Hamish Hamilton, 1967), 269.
14 Karabell, *Parting the Desert*, 177–178.
15 Winston S. Churchill, *The History of the English Speaking Peoples, Vol. 4: The Great Democracies* (Toronto: McClelland & Stewart, 1958), 293.
16 Ibid.
17 Peter Mansfield, *The British In Egypt* (New York: Holt, Rinehart and Winston, 1971), XII.
18 Said K. Aburish, *Nasser: the Last Arab* (New York: Thomas Dunne, 2004), 11–12.
19 John Gunther, *Procession* (New York: Harper and Row, 1965), 361.
20 Mansfield, *British in Egypt*, 279.
21 Mansfield, *British in Egypt*, 308.
22 Will Durant, *The Story of Civilization: Part I, Our Oriental Heritage* (New York: Simon and Schuster, 1954), 138.
23 Gamal Abdul Nasser, *Egypt's Liberation: The Philosophy of the Revolution* (Washington: Public Affairs Press, 1955), 76–77.
24 Derek Varble, *Essential Histories: The Suez Crisis 1956* (Oxford: Osprey, 2003), 13.
25 Aburish, *Nasser*, 72.
26 *Documents on Canadian External Relations*. Vol. 22, Part 1 (1956-1957), 51.
27 Keith Kyle, *Suez* (New York: St. Martin's Press, 1991), 65.
28 Kyle, *Suez*, 72.
29 Mahmoud Younes, in Donald Neff, *Warriors at Suez* (New York: The Linden Press, 1981), 269.
30 Gamal Nasser, in Kennett Love, *Suez: The Twice-Fought War* (New York: McGraw-

Hill, 1969), 347.

31 Sir Anthony Eden, *Full Circle* (London: Cassell, 1960), 424.

32 Harold Macmillan, *Riding the Storm: 1956-1959* (London: Macmillan, 1971), 101.

33 Roy Fullick and Geoffrey Powell, *Suez: The Double War* (London: Hamish Hamilton, 1979), 9.

34 Gamal Nasser, in D.R. Thorpe, *Eden* (London: Pimlico, 2004), 427.

35 Anthony Eden, in Neff, *Warriors at Suez*, 174.

36 Hugh Thomas, *The Suez Affair* (London: Weidenfeld and Nicholson, 1966), 26.

37 Neff, *Warriors at Suez*, 271.

38 Kyle, *Suez*, 137.

39 Norman Robertson to Lester Pearson, July 27, 1956. *Documents on Canadian External Relations*, 131.

40 Bertjan Verbeek, *Decision-Making in Great Britain During the Suez Crisis* (Aldershot: Ashgate, 2003), 83.

41 Anthony Eden to Louis St. Laurent, July 28, 1956. *Documents on Canadian External Relations*, 132.

42 Ibid.

43 "Nasser's Revenge," *Time* (August 6, 1956), 20.

44 Dorothy Thompson in Nasser, *Egypt's Liberation*, 5–6.

45 Neff, *Warriors at Suez*, 256.

46 John Foster Dulles in Neff, *Warriors at Suez*, 293.

47 Dwight Eisenhower in Neff, *Warriors at Suez*, 292.

48 Leonard Mosley, *Dulles* (New York: Dial/James Wade, 1978), 406.

49 Ibid.

50 Anthony Eden, in Neff, *Warriors At Suez*, 276.

51 Macmillan, *Riding the Storm*, 100.

52 Selwyn Lloyd, *Suez 1956: A Personal Account* (New York: Mayflower Books, 1978), 92.

53 Lester Pearson to Norman Robertson, July 28, 1956. *Documents on Canadian External Relations*, 133.

54 Ibid.

55 Mohamed H. Heikal, *Cutting the Lion's Tail* (New York: Arbor House, 1987), 146.

56 Anthony Nutting, *No End of a Lesson* (London: Constable, 1996), 48.

57 Ibid.

58 *Time*, August 20, 1956, 17.

59 Heikal, *Cutting the Lion's Tail*, 146.

60 Extract from Cabinet Conclusions, August 29, 1956. *Documents on Canadian External Relations*, 150.

61 Verbeek, *Decision-Making*, 90.

62 *Time*, August 20, 1956, 17.

63 Eden, *Full Circle*, 444.

64 Verbeek, *Decision-Making*, 13.

65 Eden, *Full Circle*, 448.

66 Heikal, *Cutting the Lion's Tail*, 148.

67 Heikal, *Cutting the Lion's Tail*, 149.

68 Robert Menzies, in Eden, *Full Circle*, 471.

69 Lester Pearson, *Mike*, 233.

70 Love, *Twice-Fought War*, 423.

71 Ibid.

72 Eden, *Full Circle*, 461.

73 Loyd, *Suez 1956*, 126.

74 Verbeek, *Decision-Making*, 14.

75 Lawrence Martin, *The Presidents and the Prime Ministers* (Toronto: Doubleday Canada, 1982), 15.

76 Knowlton Nash, *History on the Run* (Toronto: McClelland and Stewart, 1984), 64–65.

77 Thorpe, *Eden*, 383.

78 Verbeek, *Decision-Making*, 14.

79 Ibid.

80 Nutting, *No End of a Lesson*, 26.

81 Thorpe, *Eden*, 559–560.

82 Mosley, *Dulles*, 409.

83 Verbeek, *Decision-Making*, 14.

84 Michael Bar-Zohar, *Ben-Gurion: a Biography* (New York: Delacorte Press, 1978), 237.

85 Ibid.

86 Mordechai Bar-On, *The Gates of Gaza* (New York: St. Martin's Griffin, 1994), 235.

87 Bar-On, *Gates of Gaza*, 244.

88 Ibid.

89 Thorpe, *Eden*, 544.

90 Lloyd, *Suez 1956*, 247.

91 Lloyd, *Suez 1956*, 249.

92 Pearson to St. Laurent, September 3, 1956. *Documents on Canadian External Relations*, 154.

93 Ibid.

94 Ibid.

95 Lester Pearson, *Mike*, 232.

96 Washington telegram to Tyler Thompson, quoted by Jules Leger, August 20, 1956. *Documents on Canadian External Relations*, 107.

97 Lester Pearson, Extract from Cabinet Conclusions, August 29, 1956. Ibid. 114.

98 Lester Pearson, re. meeting with Israeli Ambassador Comay, September 11, 1956. *Documents on Canadian External Relations*, 115.

99 Lester Pearson to Permanent Representative to North Atlantic Council, September 11, 1956, 115.

100 Jules Leger to Lester Pearson, October 18, 1956. *Documents on Canadian External Relations*, 123.

101 Jules Leger to Michael Comay, January 9, 1957. *Documents on Canadian External Relations*, 130.

102 "Canadian Newsman Ordered Out of Egypt," *Globe and Mail*, August 27, 1956.

103 "Back to the Balance?" *Globe and Mail*, October 3, 1956.

104 Drew Middleton, "Anti-U.S. Feeling Grows As British Blame Dulles," *New York Times*, October 9, 1956.

105 Ibid.

106 Philip Deane, "Egyptians Seen Winning Diplomatic Victory at UN," *Globe and Mail*, October 13, 1956, 2.

107 Ibid.

108 Editorial, "Three Months," *Globe and Mail*, October 16, 1956.

109 Lord Dundee, "Strong Stand on Suez Urged by Scottish Peer," *Globe and Mail*, October 26, 1956.

110 Ibid.

111 Major-General Moshe Dayan, *Diary of the Sinai Campaign* (New York: Schocken, 1967), 38–39.

112 Dwight Eisenhower, in Bar-Zohar, *Ben Gurion*, 245.

113 Varble, *Essential Histories*, 29.

114 Varble, *Essential Histories*, 32.

115 Varble, *Essential Histories*, 33.

116 Trevor N. Dupuy, *Elusive Victory: The Arab-Israeli Wars, 1947–1974* (New York: Harper & Row, 1978), 148.

117 Dupuy, *Elusive Victory*, 154.

118 Robert Henriques, *A Hundred Hours to Suez* (New York: Viking, 1957), 65.

119 Ibid.

120 Dupuy, *Elusive Victory*, 175.

121 Robertson to Pearson, Sept. 3, 1956. *Documents on Canadian External Relations*, 154.

122 Pearson to Robertson, Sept. 29, 1956. *Documents on Canadian External Relations*, 176.

123 Varble, *Essential Histories*, 49.

124 John English, *The Worldly Years: The Life of Lester Pearson, Vol. II: 1949–1972* (Toronto: Alfred A. Knopf, 1992), 75.

125 Patricia Pearson Hannah, "My Father the Prime Minister," *Chatelaine*, September 1963, 29.

126 Osgood Caruthers, "Bombing of 4 Cities Laid to RAF, French," *New York Times*, October 31, 1956.

127 John Gale, "In Cairo, Calm," *London Observer*, October 31, 1956.

128 "Stock Prices Drop in Toronto, London and Paris," *Globe and Mail*, November 1, 1956, 1.

129 "The Middle East," *Time*, November 12, 1956, 34.

130 Aburish, *Nasser*, 112.

131 Varble, *Essential Histories*, 54.

132 W.J. Burnett, "Canadian Officer Led Raid Against Airfield in Egypt," *Globe and Mail*, November 2, 1956, 1.

133 Kyle, *Suez*, 384.

134 Kyle, *Suez*, 393.

135 Lester Pearson, *Mike*, 238.

136 Ibid.

137 Eden to St. Laurent, October 30, 1956. *Documents on Canadian External Relations*, 182.

138 Ibid.

139 Ibid.

140 Robert Bothwell, Ian Drummond, and John English, *Canada Since 1945: Power, Politics, and Provincialism* (Toronto: University of Toronto Press, 1981), 144.

141 Kyle, *Suez*, 386.

142 Bothwell et al., *Canada Since 1945*, 144.

143 Lester Pearson, *Mike*, 238.

144 St. Laurent to Eden, October 31, 1956. *Documents on Canadian External Relations*, 187.

145 Ibid.

146 Bruce Thordarson, *Lester Pearson Diplomat and Politician* (Toronto: Oxford University Press, 1974), 86.

147 Editorial, *Globe and Mail*, November 2, 1956.

148 E.S. Lavender, *Globe and Mail*, November 2, 1956.

149 Louis St. Laurent, "PM Uncertain On Suez Case; Scolds Press," *Globe and Mail*, November 2, 1956.

150 J. Harrison, *Globe and Mail*, November 5, 1956.

151 Jamieson Bone, *Globe and Mail*, November 5, 1956.

152 D.H. Mackay, *Globe and Mail*, November 5, 1956.

153 William Kirby, *Globe and Mail*, November 5, 1956.

154 R.E.K. Pemberton, *Globe and Mail*, November 5, 1956.

155 Gordon Keyes, "Fraternal Groups Support London on Suez Decision," *Globe and Mail*, November 3, 1956, 4.

156 W.F. Barfoot, in "Canadian Churchmen Sympathetic With U.K. Stand on Suez Canal," *Globe and Mail*, November 2, 1956, 4.

157 Bothwell et al., *Canada Since 1945*, 144.

158 Andre Beaufre, *The Suez Expedition 1956* (London: Faber and Faber, 1969), 103.

159 Beaufre, *Suez Expedition 1956*, 106.

160 Lester Pearson, *Mike*, 241.

161 Ibid.

162 Ibid.

163 Shadrack Mbogho, conversation with the author, January 16, 2006.

164 Norman Robertson to Lester Pearson, November 1, 1956. *Documents on Canadian External Relations*, 189.

165 Lester Pearson to Norman Robertson, October 30, 1956. *Documents on Canadian External Relations*, 180.

166 Ibid.

167 Neff, *Warriors at Suez*, 398.

168 Extract from Cabinet Conclusions, November 1, 1956. *Documents on Canadian External Relations*, 190.

169 Ibid.

170 Ibid.

171 Lester Pearson, *Mike*, 244.

172 Eden, *Full Circle*, 535–536.

173 Eden, *Full Circle*, 536.

174 Lester Pearson, *Mike*, 245.

175 Geoffrey A.H. Pearson, *Seize the Day* (Ottawa: Carleton University Press, 1993), 147.

176 Clark Davey, "PM Uncertain On Suez Case; Scolds Press," *Globe and Mail*, November 2, 1956, 17.

177 Lester Pearson, *Mike*, 246.

178 Lester Pearson, *Mike*, 247.

179 Ibid.

180 Drew Middleton, "Police Disperse Anti-Eden Mob," *The New York Times*, November 4, 1956.

181 Thorpe, *Eden*, 528.

182 Eden, *Full Circle*, 546.

183 Lloyd, *Suez 1956*, 207.

184 Middleton, "Police Disperse Anti-Eden Mob."

185 Kyle, *Suez*, 445–446.

186 Kyle, *Suez*, 446.

187 A.J. Barker, *Suez: The Seven Day War* (London: Faber and Faber, 1964), 187.

188 W.H. Lawrence, "Suez, European Crises Seen Switching Votes To 5-Star Eisenhower," *The New York Times*, November 1, 1956.

189 Kyle, *Suez*, 45.

190 Thorpe, *Eden*, 536–537.

191 Neff, *Warriors at Suez*, 403.

192 Lester Pearson, *Mike*, 249.

193 Editorial, *Globe and Mail*, November 3, 1956.

194 Ibid.

195 Extract From Cabinet Conclusions, *Documents on Canadian External Relations*, 204.

196 Ibid.

197 Lester Pearson, *Mike*, 250.

198 Lester Pearson, *Mike*, 251.

199 Desmond Morton, "Strains of Affluence 1945-1996," in Craig Brown, Ed. *The Illustrated History of Canada* (Toronto: Key Porter, 2000), 489.

200 Lester Pearson, *Mike*, 251.

201 R.A. MacKay to Lester Pearson, November 3, 1956. *Documents on Canadian External Relations*, 207.

202 Lloyd, *Suez 1956*, 203.

203 Lester Pearson, *Mike*, 252.

204 Ibid.

205 Lester Pearson, *Mike*, 253.

206 Dwight Eisenhower, *Time*, November 26, 1956, 29.

207 *Time*, November 26, 1956, 30.

208 Geoffrey A.H. Pearson, *Seize the Day*, 150.

209 Terence Robertson, *Crisis* (Toronto: McClelland and Stewart, 1964), 234–235.

210 Robertson, *Crisis*, 237.

211 Anthony Eden to Louis St. Laurent, November 5, 1956. *Documents on Canadian External Relations*, 214.

212 Robertson, *Crisis*, 232.

213 Selwyn Lloyd, in Kyle, *Suez*, 451.

214 Aneurin Bevan, in Kyle, *Suez*, 451.

215 Anthony Eden to Louis St. Laurent, November 6, 1956. *Documents on Canadian External Relations*, 222.

216 Anthony Eden to Louis St. Laurent, November 5, 1956. *Documents on Canadian External Relations*, 215.

217 Hugh Thomas, *The Suez Affair* (London: Weidenfeld and Nicholson, 1967), 143.

218 Colonel Trevor N. Dupuy, *Elusive Victory* (Harper & Row, 1978), 206.

219 Dupuy, *Elusive Victory*, 206.

220 Barker, *Seven Day War*, 152.

221 Beaufre, *Suez Expedition 1956*, 110.

222 Varble, *Essential Histories*, 77.

223 Thomas, *Suez Affair*, 142.

224 Barker, *Seven Day War*, 141.

225 Doctor Sandy Cavanagh, in Love, *Twice-Fought War*, 620.

226 Frank White, *Time*, November 19, 1956, 31.

227 Kyle, *Suez*, 462.

228 Pierre Leulliette, in Love, *Twice-Fought War*, 601.

229 Varble, *Essential Histories*, 66.

230 Fullick and Powell, *Double War*, 156.

231 Pierre Leulliette, in Love, *Twice-Fought War*, 655.

232 Sandy Cavanagh, in Love, *Twice-Fought War*, 655.

233 Beaufre, *Suez Expedition 1956*, 115.

234 Kyle, *Suez*, 491.

235 Ibid.

236 Dwight Eisenhower, November 7, 1956. "Extract from Cabinet Conclusions." *Documents on Canadian External Relations*, 232.

237 Ibid.

238 Editorial, *Globe and Mail*, November 9, 1956.

239 Editorial, *Globe and Mail*, November 12, 1956.

240 Doug and Ron McEwen, *Globe and Mail*, November 9, 1956.

241 Blair Fraser, "Backstage at Ottawa," *Maclean's*, November 10, 1956, 10.

242 Ibid.

243 Lester Pearson, *Mike*, 260.

244 John Holmes, "Memorandum by Assistant Under-Secretary of State for External Affairs," November 12, 1956, *Documents on Canadian External Relations*, 245.

245 Lester Pearson, *Documents on Canadian External Relations*, 245.

246 Ibid.

247 Desmond Morton, *A Military History of Canada* (Edmonton: Hurtig Publishers, 1985), 241–2.

248 Lester Pearson, *Mike*, 261–2.

249 Kyle, *Suez*, 481.

250 Nutting, *No End of a Lesson*, 134.

251 Patrick O'Donovan, *London Observer*, November 9, 1956.

252 J. Chester Ede, "Canada's Prestige Seen Advanced in Crisis," *Globe and Mail*, November 12, 1956, 4.

253 Charles A. Wunder, *Globe and Mail*, November 12, 1956, 4..

254 Editorial, the *Halifax Chronicle-Herald*, December 12, 1956.

255 Sean M. Maloney, *Canada and UN Peacekeeping* (St. Catherines: Vanwell, 2002), 81.

256 Ibid.

257 Maloney, *Peacekeeping*, 134.

258 Howard Green, in Lester Pearson, *Mike*, 273.

259 Eden, *Full Circle*, 581–2.

260 Ibid.

261 *Time*, November 19, 1956, 39.

262 Rab Butler, *Time*, December 3, 1956, 27.

263 Anthony Eden, *Time*, December 3, 1956, 27.

264 Editorial, *Globe and Mail*, November 20, 1956.

265 Editorial, *Globe and Mail*, November 21, 1956.

266 Robert C. Doty, "Mob Shouts for Nasser in Port Said," *The New York Times*, November 21, 1956.

267 Dave McIntosh, "Canadians Get Taste of Egyptian Desert Sand," *Halifax Chronicle-Herald*, December 13, 1956.

268 Ibid.

269 Maloney, *Peacekeeping*, 73.

270 "Speed Troop Withdrawal From Suez," *Halifax Chronicle-Herald*, December 5, 1956, 1.

271 Varble, *Essential Histories*, 82.

272 *Time*, November 19, 1956, 21.

273 Maloney, *Peacekeeping*, 71.

274 David Ben Gurion, speech to Israeli Knesset, November 7, 1956, in Bar-Zohar, *Ben-Gurion*, 249.

275 Golda Meier, January 7, 1956. [R.A.] Mac Kay to Lester B. Pearson, *Documents on Canadian External Relations*, 339.

276 Eden, *Full Circle*, 569.

277 Norman Robertson to Lester Pearson, December 13, 1956, *Documents on Canadian External Relations*, 307.

278 Ibid.

279 Reuters, "Eden's Absence Stirs Speculation On Leadership," *The Halifax Chronicle-Herald*, December 6, 1956, 2.

280 Lester Pearson to Louis St. Laurent, December 18, 1956, *Documents on Canadian External Relations*, 320.

281 Lloyd, *Suez 1956*, 237.

282 Lt.-Gen. E.L.M. Burns, *Between Arab and Israeli* (Toronto: Clarke, Irwin, 1962), 239.

283 Dave McIntosh, *Halifax Chronicle-Herald*, December 15, 1956.

284 Peter Worthington, *Looking For Trouble* (Toronto: Key Porter, 1984), 48.

285 Fred Gaffen, *In the Eye of the Storm* (Ottawa: Deneau & Wayne, 1987), 46.

286 Ibid.

287 Burns, *Arab and Israeli*, 236.

288 Lloyd, *Suez 1956*, 235–236.

289 Burns, *Arab and Israeli*, 258.

290 Maloney, *Peacekeeping*, 75.

291 Gaffen, *Eye of the Storm*, 52.

292 Burns, *Arab and Israeli*, 275.

293 Bill Lemaire, author interview, October 28, 2005.

294 Maloney, *Peacekeeping*, 75.

295 Gaffen, *Eye of the Storm*, 227.

296 H.C. Fielding, author interview, September 24, 2005.

297 Brian Urquhart, *A Life In Peace and War* (New York: Harper & Row, 1987), 138.

298 Michael Harbottle, *The Blue Berets* (London: Leo Cooper, 1971), 8.

299 Michael Kovrig, author interview, January 16, 2006.